JERE E. BROPHY

CAROLYN M. EVERTSON

The University of Texas at Austin

Learning from Teaching
A Developmental Perspective

Allyn and Bacon, Inc.

Boston · London · Sydney

Library of Congress Cataloging in Publication Data

Brophy, Jere E
    Learning from teaching.

    Bibliography: p. 197-201.
    Includes index.
    1. Teacher-student relationships. 2. Interaction analysis in education. 3. Teaching. I. Evertson, Carolyn M., 1935– joint author. II. Title.
LB1033.B66   371.1'02   75-30502
ISBN 0-205-05013-1   *(paperbound)*
ISBN 0-205-05488-9   *(hardbound)*

To our parents

Contents

Preface

The history of the field of education is marked by fadism. Ideas and practices are introduced by strong advocates who make impressive claims for their effectiveness, and the ideas or practices are accepted enthusiastically on the basis of these claims, despite the lack of supporting research. Typically, the innovations last a few years and then come under attack by new advocates who support with equal or greater fervor a different and sometimes even contradictory approach. Teachers who have been on the job a long time are all too familiar with this process, having seen the very same idea come into and go out of vogue two or three separate times during their careers.

All of this would be amusing if it were not so destructive to teacher morale and to the process of building up a data base that would establish teaching as an applied science, in which professionals put into practice a set of well established principles with confidence that they will have reasonably predictable and satisfactory success. This is what teaching should be, in our view, but at present it is a goal, not a reality. Undergraduate education majors all too frequently learn only a smattering of principles and methods, many of which are vague and some of which are contradictory. Depending upon when they are in school, the content of what they learn is likely to be heavily biased toward whatever is popular at the moment.

Typically, when they begin student teaching, they find that little of what they learned in their teacher education courses is clearly applicable, so that they end up imitating what their supervising teachers do. This is of more practical usefulness than their earlier experiences, although the quality of what they learn in this apprenticeship role is directly dependent upon the skills of the supervising teacher. Furthermore, most student teachers get to work with only one supervising teacher, so that they do not get to see a wide range of teaching styles or have an opportunity to rationally select styles that are most suitable to them.

All of this is doubly unfortunate, because there have been great advances in the technology of teacher education. In addition to the traditional textbooks and related exercises, teacher education programs now typically feature such powerful instructional devices as group learning activities, role playing, and video taped lessons with opportunities to observe and get feedback. Thus, at present we know a great deal about *how* to educate future teachers, but we know relatively little about *what* to tell them to do. The content of teacher education programs still is made up largely of principles and practices enjoying present popularity because of strong advocacy rather than because they have demonstrated effectiveness and are backed by a research base to establish their validity.

Unfortunately, one of the presently popular fads related to education is bitter criticism of schools and teachers. A seemingly endless parade of popular books and articles has appeared over the past several years suggesting that schools are at best stodgy and out-moded and at worst prison-like institutions that force unhappy and unwilling students to endure pointless activities and experiences. Similarly, teachers typically are featured as bumbling and ineffectual at best and cynical and sadistic at worst. The continued publication of these cheap shots would be bad enough, but much to our surprise, the educational establishment, including many teachers, has received such abuse without protest and in many cases with positive enthusiasm.

This is a continuing source of amazement to us, because, although we have seen a few miserable schools and horrible teachers, on the whole we believe that schools are doing a reasonably good job and that the average teacher is a dedicated individual concerned about not only student learning but student development in all areas of living. Furthermore, we find that the average teacher usually has more direct personal knowledge, and certainly more knowledge concerning solutions to problems, than do the strident critics who are very good at delineating problems but very weak on offering solutions.

In any case, we believe that education needs less heat and more light. Educational problems will *not* be solved by heaping criticism on schools and teachers, or by advocating new ideas and techniques without first showing that they really work. School administrators and teachers do not need further abuse; they need specific, data based information that will enable them to diagnose particular situations accurately and follow through with "treatment" established as effective or at least probably effective in such situations.

This is what a medical doctor or other professional working in an applied science does. Teachers are severely limited in their ability to do it, however, because the necessary data base that would provide the specialized knowledge and expertise needed in order to proceed in such a systematic fashion is largely non-existent. Educational researchers have not come up with very many dependable relationships be· tween particular situations, particular teacher behavior, and particular student outcomes. As a result, the teacher must rely on a combination of experience and "seat of the pants" creativity in trying to decide how to handle a particular situation.

The research to be described in this book represents an attempt to alleviate this problem to some degree by adding significantly to the data base available to teachers, particularly teachers who are working in the early elementary school grades. Although research by a variety of investigators will be discussed, the book concentrates on the findings of a large scale, two-year field observation study of second and third grade teachers (called the Texas Teacher Effectiveness Project).

The study was unique in many ways, combining aspects of teacher selection, data gathering, and data analyses innovations designed to help overcome the complexities involved in field studies conducted in real classrooms and to increase the likelihood that useful results would emerge. Perhaps the single most important aspect of the study was that it was conducted by observing experienced teachers engaged in their

usual activities with their regular students in their everyday
classrooms, something that might seem natural and logical
for an educational research project but which has been
surprisingly infrequent to date.

In any case, although the study was by no means an
unqualified success, it did produce a wealth of information
which should be of immediate use to teachers and which
should help both in-service and pre-service teachers to appreciate the need for a data base to establish the validity of even
the most popular and widely advocated techniques. Many of
our findings provide support for the ideas presented in teacher
education textbooks, but many others, perhaps a majority,
provide no support for such ideas or even flatly contradict
them.

The findings are presented in a non-technical fashion for
readers interested in the main findings and implications.
Only those findings which were statistically significant and
which replicated over the two separate years of study are
presented. This selective presentation is used in order to
facilitate communication. The study involved a very large
number of variables and some complex statistical analyses
techniques which yielded voluminous and complicated tables
and graphs presenting the findings. Partly because of their
complexity, but mostly because of their sheer volume, most
tables and graphs have been excluded from this book. However, readers interested in detailed presentations of data are
provided with references to a series of research reports containing all of the relevant information.

As will be clear upon reading, the book presents several
fundamental conclusions and implications about teacher education and about the nature of teaching, particularly teaching
young children in the early elementary grades. Part of the
rationale for publishing it in this form is to publicize these
important and to some degree controversial ideas to educators
at large. However, the more specific purpose of the book is
its potential as a teaching vehicle. It should be useful as a
textbook or textbook adjunct in teacher education courses,
particularly for teachers intending to work with elementary
school children. It also should be useful to in-service teachers
for individual reading, in-service workshops, or graduate

courses designed for continuing education. Finally, beacuse of the issues it raises and the methodological approaches it describes, the book should be useful to practitioners and course instructors in such fields as educational research, educational psychology, curriculum and instruction, child psychology, learning psychology, and related fields.

Acknowledgments

The research data preparation, data analysis, and writing activities involved in the preparation of this book required almost five years of effort on the part of a large number of individuals, which in turn was made possible by the funding agencies which supported the project and the administrators who helped facilitate this support. The research was supported for several years by the U.S. Office of Education Contract OE 6-10-108, The Research and Development Center for Teacher Education at the University of Texas at Austin (Oliver H. Bown and Robert F. Peck, co-directors). More recently the project has been supported by a National Institute of Education grant NIE-C-74-0089, The Correlates of Effective Teaching (Jere E. Brophy, Principal Investigator; Carolyn M. Evertson, Project Director). The confidence and support of these funding agencies who made the study possible, and particularly of the specific individuals involved, is deeply appreciated. We must note, however, that the opinions expressed herein are the authors'. They do not necessarily reflect the position or policy of the Office of Education or of the National Institute of Education, and no official endorsement by these agencies should be inferred.

We also wish to acknowledge and thank Dr. Thomas Good and Dr. Donald Veldman for their suggestions regarding the overall conceptualization of the research; Dr. Edmund Emmer, Dr. Earl Jennings, and Dr. Donald Veldman, for their statistical design suggestions; and Dr. Edmund Emmer, Dr. Thomas Good, and Dr. Barak Rosenshine for their critical comments and suggestions. Also, we wish to acknowledge and thank our friends and colleagues in The Research and Development Center for Teacher Education at the University of Texas at Austin for providing the

kinds of general encouragement and support that are necessary to make an undertaking of this magnitude possible.

A special note of thanks is extended to the Austin
Independent School District. This study made unusually large
demands upon the resources of teachers and administrators
involved in the day to day operation of a city school system,
but they nevertheless responded with continuous and facilita-
tive cooperation. Special appreciation is extended to Marshel
Ashley, Dr. Freda Holley, and Dr. Matthew Snapp, who
helped us work out the details involved in getting the study
underway and in seeing it through to its conclusion.

Needless to say, our deepest appreciation goes to the
principals and particularly the teachers involved in the study,
who went out of their way to help in every way they could
with a study that required them to "live in a fish bowl" for
as long as two years. Their dedication and professionalism
serve as an example to us and to educators everywhere.

Obviously, a project of this scope cannot be accomplished without a large and competent group of research
associates and staff. Fortunately, we were assisted in this
effort by numerous hard working and talented individuals.
Those who played a significant role in the data collection and
analyses and/or in the preparation of this book include the
following:

Connie Anderson, Dr. Shyam Ahuja, Maria Buczynski,
W. John Crawford, Carol King, Karen Mays, Dr. Mark Mays,
Nancy Moore, Dr. Piara Pannu, Kathey Paredes, Brian Peck,
Dr. Teresa Peck, Dr. Kathleen Senior, Carol Watkins,
Dr. Michael Weissberg, and Andrea Winter, who observed in
classrooms and helped prepare data for analysis;

Michael Baum, James Blackwell, Cynthia Coulter, Bucky
Evertson, Carol Greenhalgh, Janet Honea, Mary Jane Leahy,
Linda Mahaffey, Jane Ogden, Gael Sherman, Mike Tebeleff,
and Ann Turney, who helped prepare data for analysis;

John Brozovsky, W. John Crawford, Marc McGee,
Brian Peck, Jon Sheffield, James Sherrill, and Wally Washington, who were involved in programming and statistical
analyses of the data; and

Susan Florence, Janet Honea, Karen Mays, Beatrice
Mladenka, Gwen Newman, Marilyn Turner, Jean Waltman,

and Sidney Weaver, who assisted in manuscript preparation

Special recognition is extended to W. John Crawford, Carol King, Nancy Moore, Gwen Newman, Brian Peck, and Dr. Teresa Peck, who assumed major responsibilities for the project as a whole.

Regarding the development of this particular book into its final form, we wish to acknowledge the encouragement and specific suggestions of R. Curtis Whitesel, our editor, and of the four anonymous reviewers who all made helpful suggestions. We also wish to thank Arlene Brophy and Dr. Thomas Good for reading an earlier draft of the book and making useful suggestions for improvement.

Most importantly we wish to express our deepest appreciation to the teachers we learned from. Obviously, this refers primarily to the teachers that we studied in the process of carrying out this research, but it also includes the teachers who taught us during our own development and other teachers who have influenced us in one way or another. In this connection, we wish to specifically single out Sara F. Smith, whose career provides a model of professionalism and dedication for all who know her.

Finally, we wish to dedicate the book to our parents, Eileen and Joseph Brophy and Jane and Carl Miller, who were our first and most important teachers.

The Question of Teacher Effectiveness

1

Gwen Newman is flustered. She is into her third month of attempting to teach second grade children in a lower-class urban school, and still nothing is going right. She had been afraid of this from the moment she heard her school assignment. She had come from a middle-class background and had attended middle-class schools herself as a child, and her observations and practice teaching experiences also were in middle-class schools.

She had read material about lower-class and minority group children in various courses, but she had had no direct experience teaching them before she began the school year. She was idealistic and dedicated, however, and she began the school year with determination to work hard and do well. She carefully reviewed what she was taught in college, carefully went through the second grade curriculum, and talked to the principal and several teachers at the school in an effort to make sure that she was really ready when school started.

Things went well in some ways. In particular, she was well accepted by the children despite her fears that she might not be, and despite the fact that she sometimes found herself "cracking down" on them, even though she had been taught that teachers shouldn't have to do this. However, the problems far outweighed the successes. In short, the kids weren't learning. Even though Gwen took care to apply everything she had been taught and to follow the procedures prescribed in the teacher handbooks carefully, it was clear that she wasn't succeeding. Many kids were progressing only very slowly and with great difficulty, and many already had failed so totally and consistently that they had become turned off on school. Often she couldn't succeed in teaching the material in a lesson even if she repeated it several times. What was the problem?

Mr. and Mrs. Crawford weren't sure what to think when they found out that their son, Johnny, was assigned to Miss Coulter's class for third grade. At first they had been quite pleased, because several neighbors with children two years older than Johnny were unanimous in praising Miss Coulter as a personable and effective teacher who would do a good job with Johnny. However, Johnny complained that children in the grade ahead of him who had had Miss Coulter the previous year were always complaining that she was mean. Were the parents and the children using different criteria in judging Miss Coulter? Had Miss Coulter changed drastically in the last year? What should they say and do if Johnny asks them to try to get him transferred to another class?

Jane Ogden enjoyed her job as school principal, and she was good at it. Although each day offered many new problems, she found herself able to cope with most of them effectively and relatively easily. However, one day the school district presented her with a problem that she didn't feel competent to handle: evaluating her teaching staff. It was not that Jane feared evaluations. She felt comfortable giving both praise and constructive criticism to her teachers, and the teachers seemed to appreciate and benefit from her efforts. However, these informal and individualized evaluations were very different from filling out the evaluation forms that the school district had sent to her.

The school district wanted her to rank her teachers on general effectiveness. How was she to do this? What criteria should she use? Miss Sherman had one pattern of strengths and weaknesses, Miss Mahaffey had another, and Mr. Washington had a third. She respected each of these teachers and felt that each was valuable, but in different ways and for different reasons. She saw no way to rank them or even to describe their "general effectiveness," whatever *that* meant. Nevertheless, the school district required her to do so, and her evaluations might affect their careers. Obviously, then she had to do everything possible to insure that those evaluations were objective and thorough. But how?

These three vignettes are fictional, but typical. They illustrate a major problem that exists in education at all levels from preschool through graduate school. Everyone has *opinions* about what good teaching is, and most people tend to think that they *know* what good teaching is. However, when you get down to specific cases, things that seem simple and clear can turn out to be frustratingly difficult and ambiguous.

One problem is lack of agreement about **criteria.** One teacher produces good learning gains but uses authoritarian classroom management methods that frighten many children and turn off most of the rest. Another teacher is very warm and child-oriented, so that her students love her and love school generally. However, they don't learn very much compared to children taught by the first teacher. Which of these two teachers is better? The answer depends upon your general values and your specific opinions on such issues as the roles of teachers and students and the nature of schooling.

Even with clear criteria, though, fair and objective judgments are hard to make because of inconsistencies and complexities. For various reasons, most of them still unknown, many teachers are *inconsistent* from one year to the next in the degree of success they achieve in producing student learning gains, in the emotional responses they produce in students, and in their own emotional reactions and general behavior in the classroom. Many of the most inconsistent teachers are new teachers who are learning on the job and changing gradually over a period of years. However, only a minority of experienced teachers who might be expected to have settled into predictable patterns of behavior actually do show consistency in their relative success in producing student learning gains from one year to the next (Brophy, 1973).

Teachers probably are somewhat more consistent in their general affective behavior (warmth, enthusiasm, student orientation, authoritarian punitiveness, and the like). However, teachers' moods and morale can be affected by agreeable or disagreeable aspects of their personal lives outside of school, and also by factors inside the school such as the number and kinds of students in their classes in a particular year, the arrival of a new principal, or the adoption of a new curriculum. Thus, even though most teachers have fairly well established reputations around the school which "describe" what they are like (at least, most of us think that such reputations exist), research on student attitudes has shown that they have surprisingly low stability from one year to the next (Good and Grouws, 1975). A teacher who is popular this year may not be popular next year.

We could go on to take up additional considerations, but perhaps this is a good place to make a brief statement that summarizes the implications of these considerations and forms the rationale for the research described in this book. That is, despite thousands of research studies, books, and articles, there is still little or no agreement about what good teaching is!

Weak Research Base

Part of the problem is that, although much educational research has been conducted, not much of it has been designed to identify effective teaching behavior. Many studies were confined to questionnaires or other methods of collecting data on teacher opinions. Few such studies were concerned with teacher effectiveness, and those that were tended to use criteria such as ratings by principals or supervisors, or designations by someone else, that the teacher involved was a "master" teacher. This approach might have produced useful findings, except for one fatal weakness: ratings of teaching effectiveness and designations of individuals as "master" teachers are notoriously unreliable. Different raters use different criteria and tend to be biased in making their ratings, so that ratings rarely agree with much consistency, certainly not enough to justify their use as criteria for characterizing teachers.

Even research using more objective criteria of effectiveness, such as teacher success in producing student learning gains, has been rather unproductive. One reason for this is that much of it has focused on attempting to validate new curricula or methods. Such studies usually involved comparing the learning gains of students taught by teachers using the innovative curriculum or method with the gains of students taught with traditional methods. Unfortunately, the vast majority of such studies have shown *no* significant differences between groups.

Furthermore, even when significant differences were obtained, such studies practically never included observations of the teachers' classroom behavior, so that usually it is not clear why the group that did better got better results. It *may* have been because the teachers in the experimental group were using the new curriculum or method appropriately, and that it really was superior to traditional ones. However, this is only one of many possible explanations. For example, it is not safe to assume that the experimental teachers were using the new curriculum or method the way they were supposed to be using it. The few studies which have been designed to include observation of the degree to which teachers actually implemented the new curriculum or method according to their instructions have yielded very mixed results. Many revealed that the experimental teachers failed to follow their instructions very faithfully.

Also, it cannot safely be assumed that teachers in the control group systematically teach differently than teachers in the experimental group. Where the experiment involves particular teaching methods, teachers in the control group may use these methods spontaneously even though the experimenters do not give them any special instructions. Even when the experiment involves a new curriculum, teachers in the control group may be supplementing the traditional curriculum with materials or activities very similar to those used in the experimental curriculum. Factors such as these probably are responsible for a large proportion of the results showing no significant advantage to the experimental curriculum or method.

However, even where significant differences are obtained, they cannot necessarily be attributed to the experimental program. Results favoring experimental groups over control groups often are due to what have been called "Hawthorne effects." These are effects of increased enthusiasm and expectations which result from being part of an experimental innovation. When teachers and students are in an experimental group using a new curriculum or method which they are led to believe is superior to traditional curricula or methods, they usually show increased enthusiasm and morale because they have been lucky enough to be chosen for the experimental group. Unless precautions were taken to control for this extra motivation in the experimental group (and usually such precautions were not taken), it is reasonable to suppose that some if not all of the advantage shown by the experimental group was due simply to Hawthorne effects rather than to any significant difference which makes the new curricula or methods significantly better than the old ones.

In summary, a major problem hindering the search for effective teaching behavior has been the small percentage of educational studies which have looked at teacher behavior systematically. Many studies were confined to questionnaires or interviews designed to gather only opinion data, and most of the studies designed to document the effectiveness of particular curricula or methods did not include observation of the teachers and therefore did not produce information about the relationships between teacher behavior and student outcomes. Among studies which did include systematic teacher observations, an additional problem is that a large proportion were conducted in laboratory experiments or in micro-teaching studies requiring a future teacher to present a short videotaped lesson to a few classmates. Such studies have yielded certain consistent relationships between teacher behavior and student outcomes (Dunkin and Biddle, 1974; Rosenshine and Furst, 1973), but these relationships have not held up as well in the classroom as they have in the laboratory. Thus, compounding the shortage of data on teacher behavior in general, there is a particular shortage of data on teacher behavior in naturalistic teaching situations (real classrooms).

The Cult of Criticism

The absence of solid data on effective teaching has not discouraged well meaning but usually misguided activists from advocating change, often writing in purple prose laden with moralistic zeal or righteous paternalism. In fact, picking on schools and teachers, cataloging their real or imagined failures, has been a popular formula for writing best-selling books about education in recent years. In fairness, we should acknowledge that certain of these books have been instrumental in helping correct unfortunate situations in particular school districts and even in the country at large, so that they do have some value in calling attention to undesirable practices that should be avoided. However, this is relatively easy to do. It is always much simpler to state what is wrong and identify what one *should not do* than it is to offer prescriptive solutions to problems by gathering information on what one *should do*. The research to be described in this book has this positive, prescriptive orientation.

An especially unfortunate tendency in these negativistic books has been to heap blame upon teachers, holding them responsible for virtually everything that might be wrong with schools. This is incorrect and unjust. First, teachers often are expected to correct problems which they did not create, do not in any way control, and cannot reasonably be expected to remedy. Second, even in areas where teachers can reasonably be expected to solve problems, they often are hamstrung or overwhelmed by too many responsibilities, conflicting demands, administrative red tape, insufficient assistance or resources, and the like. Third, as noted above, educational research has not yet produced a data base that teachers can turn to for dependable information about how to handle their problems. These problems are many and mostly well known, but proposed solution strategies are few and usually unreliable. This is why experiences similar to those of Gwen Newman, the fictional teacher in the first vignette at the beginning of this chapter, are so common.

Teachers as Unimportant and Ineffective

Ironically, in addition to books denouncing teachers for having undesirable effects, probably the next most popular formula for a best-selling book about education in recent years has been an attempt to show that schools (and presumably teachers) have no measurable effect at all. Such writers view education as controlled entirely by the student, with the teacher playing a relatively minor role as babysitter and provider of materials and input. This theoretical position received some indirect support from studies showing that measures of the quality of a school's teaching staff usually do not add much if any significance to predictions of student learning over and beyond what can be achieved by predicting from measures of student ability and/or social status alone. The most famous of these studies have been the so-called "Coleman Report," (Coleman et al., 1966) and several re-analyses of its original data, although numerous other studies have produced essentially the same results.

   These studies are open to a variety of criticisms concerning bias in their samples and the use of inappropriate statistics. However, a more important criticism is that their basic design virtually insures the findings described above, masking rather than revealing teacher effects. First, the data collected on teachers in such studies were restricted to information available in records, such as sources and kinds of academic degrees, years of experience, and scores on national teachers' examinations. Such variables seemed (and were) sensible as indicators of the quality of a school's teaching staff in the early studies, but later research established that they do not correlate much if at all with either the teachers' classroom behavior or their success in producing student learning gains. Thus, this "information" about the "quality" of school faculties really was no information at all.

Also, school faculties are composed of individual teachers who range from very poor to very good. By analyzing the data according to *schools*, investigators mixed together the effects of good, bad, and mediocre teachers, thus masking rather than revealing the effects of contrasting teaching quality upon student learning. Teacher effects can be assessed only when teachers are studied individually, not lumped together as a school faculty.

Finally, due to a combination of *de facto* segregation of schools and *de facto* assignment of better teachers to higher social class schools, it is extremely likely that the most talented students were getting the highest quality teaching, and vice versa.

Taken together, these factors virtually insured that studies using schools rather than individual teachers as their unit of analysis would fail to find any measurable teacher effects (for an extended discussion of these studies, see Good, Biddle, and Brophy, 1975). More appropriately designed studies which use the individual teacher as the unit of analysis have shown that both statistically and practically significant teacher differences exist even when student abilities have been taken into account (Brophy, 1973; Veldman and Brophy, 1974). What is needed now are studies that systematically record what teachers do in the classroom and relate these behavioral data to measures of student outcomes. In this way, a data base can be built up specifying the relationships between teacher behavior and student outcomes and providing prescriptive implications for what teachers should do in certain situations. This was the intent of the research to be described.

Identifying Effective Teaching

In summary, then, the present research was designed to begin to fill the gaps in the existing literature by systematically measuring teacher behavior and relating it to student outcomes. The study was not an experiment designed to test particular hypotheses. Instead, it was an observational study designed to reveal relationships between naturally occurring teacher behavior and student outcomes, using a sample of experienced teachers with records of consistency in their relative success in producing student learning gains. Data were taken in each of two consecutive years by coding teacher-student interaction as it occurred spontaneously in the classrooms in which these experienced teachers were teaching their regular students the regular curriculum.

Thus, in an effort to insure that the findings would be representative of classroom teaching and would generalize to other classrooms, the research focused on: (a) the study of experienced teachers with records of consistency in relative effectiveness (as opposed to student teachers, first year teachers, or inconsistent teachers); (b) the coding of naturalistic teacher-student interaction as it occurred in the classrooms by coders recording data on the spot (as opposed to coding teachers attempting to install a new curriculum or to follow experimental procedures, and also as opposed to disrupting the naturalistic situation through video taping); and (c) the use of a sophisticated coding system that recorded a large number of different kinds of teacher-student interactions and took into account certain contextual differences (concerning when and how interactions occurred) and certain aspects of interaction sequence (teacher initiated vs. student initiated; sequences of action and reaction).

This approach was developed on the bases of earlier observations of and discussions with teachers. These were designed to identify classroom interaction sequences and contextual differences that could be observed by coders and that were important to teachers. Thus, the observation system was developed on the basis of classroom experiences for use in classroom research (as opposed to the use of methods developed for psychological laboratory research, which often are not appropriate for use in the classroom). This reflects our belief that educational researchers must develop their own variables, measurement methods, and research procedures if they are to be effective in providing the data base that education needs. Techniques borrowed directly from other social sciences are useful for many subproblems involved in this larger effort, of course, but educational research ultimately will have to stand on its own if it is to get the job done. Hopefully, the present study represents a forward step in this effort.

Details of the research methods and statistical analyses used in the study are provided in Appendices A and B. Readers interested in possessing this information before reading the results of the study should turn to Appendices A and B before continuing with the rest of the book. It is not necessary to read these appendices in order to understand the results, but it is necessary to do so in order to evaluate the results and the study as a whole. Thus, we recommend that all readers read this material at some point. In addition to the material contained in these two appendices, Appendix C consists of an annotated bibliography of more technical reports that contain data tables and much more detailed and specific information than is available in the present volume. Readers interested in information at this level of detail are referred to these sources.

Stated most simply, this research involved analyzing the relationships between teacher characteristics and student learning on standardized achievement tests of language arts (word knowledge, word discrimination, and reading) and mathematics (arithmetic computation and arithmetic reasoning). This means that our definition of teacher effectiveness boils down to **effectiveness in producing student learning gains** on these tests. This skill is almost universally recognized as important for teachers in general and especially for teachers working in the early elementary grades, but it should be obvious that it is only one of many possible criteria of teacher effectiveness. Thus, readers should remain aware as they go through the rest of the book that our use of terms like "teacher effectiveness" and "effective teacher" refers *only* to teacher ability to produce student learning gains. This is important, not only because of the disagreement about criteria of effectiveness discussed previously, but also because many of our own findings, as well as findings by other investigators, suggest that certain teacher behavior that fosters learning has a negative effect upon student morale and attitudes. This problem will be pointed out and discussed in several places in the book.

Bearing in mind that our definition of teacher effectiveness was restricted to teacher success in producing student learning gains, let us turn to the data to see what kind of teacher characteristics were associated with such effectiveness.

The study was carried out in the classrooms of second and third grade teachers who were unusually consistent, year after year, in their relative effectiveness (See Appendix A for details about how they were identified). We will begin the discussion of our findings with descriptions of these highly consistent teachers, describing both how they resembled and how they differed from other teachers working in the same school system at the same grade levels.

What the Teachers Were Like

2

Our initial impression of the teachers in the sample was that they were a very heterogeneous group. They seemed to differ from a random sample of second and third grade teachers in the school district only by virtue of their consistency in producing student learning gains on standardized achievement tests and their higher than average ages and years of teaching experience. Both of the latter differences, of course, were directly related to our selection procedures. That is, since we had restricted the study to teachers with at least four consecutive years of experience teaching at their particular grade level, we had virtually insured that the teachers in the study would be somewhat older than average and have more teaching experience than average. This proved to be the case.

The fact that these teachers were older

than average and had more years of experience teaching at
their grade level, in addition to the fact that they were
consistent across time in effectiveness as compared to other
teachers who were not, opened up the possibility that there
might be other characteristics unique to this teacher sample
which should be identified and taken into account in assessing the results. Such knowledge would be important in
generalizing the findings to other teachers.

We knew in advance, of course, that teachers in the
sample would probably be somewhat older and have somewhat greater experience than average. However, we considered this to be a plus factor that would increase the
appropriateness of such a group for the study and not pose
a significant problem with regard to the generalization of
results. Consequently, we selected the sample as we did.

The fact that these teachers also were particularly consistent in their relative success in producing student learning
gains was a somewhat different matter. This made them especially appropriate for a study designed to identify the
correlates of the ability to produce student learning gains,
but it also was a quality that made these teachers different
from other teachers. Because we did not see any other obvious differences and could not think of anything in particular that "should" be associated with consistency as such (as
opposed to consistent high success vs. consistent low success,
about which we did have some hypotheses), we assumed that
consistent teachers would not differ from other teachers
in any other systematic ways.

However, this was an assumption. In order to check it
systematically, we compared the responses of the teachers
in our sample to those of a random sample of 38 second and
third grade teachers from the same school district who agreed
to fill out 495-item questionnaires (for a ten dollar reim-
bursement).

These analyses produced mixed results. On the whole,
the two samples of teachers were much more similar than
different. Nevertheless, significant differences (beyond the
.05 level) appeared for 57 of the 495 items, when only
about 25 items should have shown differences at this level
of significance by chance alone. These differences will be

discussed in a later section, following discussion of items on which all teachers agreed or disagreed.

Figure 2-1 (on page 28) shows the 58 items upon which all or almost all of the teachers in the entire sample or in one of the two SES (socioeconomic status) subgroups agreed. These items were excluded from later analyses because they showed no variance within the sample or because variance was extremely low (no more than five teachers had scores different from the others). Where agreement was unanimous or near-unanimous for the total sample of teachers, the word "total" appears in parentheses following the item on Figure 2-1. Items which elicited general agreement but still showed enough variance to allow analyses within one of the two SES groups also are included in Figure 2-1. Those items which are followed by the words "High SES Only" in parentheses are items that teachers working in high SES schools were unanimous or near-unanimous in agreeing with. Similarly, items followed by the words "Low SES Only" in parentheses are items that teachers working in low SES schools were unanimous or near unanimous in agreeing with.

Inspection of Figure 2-1 reveals that the items cover a broad range of beliefs, attitudes, and practices (as reported by the teachers). Many are susceptible to social desirability influences, in that it is rather obvious that agreement would be expected on the basis of what is commonly considered good teaching practice (children should enjoy school and should work on their own; teachers should be well prepared; cooperation with the home and rapport with the students is important; regular use of praise is good; teachers should have such traits as patience, the ability to be interesting as well as informative, and the willingness to admit their ignorance).

However, other items which did not have this social desirability feature also pulled high agreement, including some that might have been expected to pull disagreement (taking neatness into account when grading assignments, aiming instructional level toward middle achievers, asserting that more time to relax and think was needed, stress on facts over generalizations, endorsement of daily reviews, endorsement of ability grouping, and several others). Nevertheless, it is true that most teachers would agree with most of the items included on Figure 2-1, so that it contains few surprises.

There were some interesting differences between the responses of teachers from high SES schools compared to those from low SES schools, although it should be kept in mind that the differences sometimes reflect only strong agreement versus weaker agreement, and not necessarily agreement versus disagreement. In any case, the responses of the high SES teachers seemed to be somewhat more suspect on grounds of social desirability, and also to be somewhat more traditional. They also reflected certain major ideas common in teacher education, especially the concepts involved in indirect teaching and curiosity learning.

Teachers from high SES schools were unanimous or near-unanimous in stressing the importance of allowing students to call out comments, providing enrichment materials, building good rapport with students, praising frequently, using peer tutoring, keeping interest high, avoiding rote memorization, asking questions frequently, and avoiding doing too much lecturing or other direct teaching that might hurt student interest or make them overly passive learners. Responses by the high SES teachers to this set of items present a consistent picture of child orientation, warmth, and philosophical commitment to teaching through indirect, child-discovery approaches. However, much of ths was contradicted by the responses of these same teachers to other items, as well as by several aspects of their classroom behavior. For example, despite the picture of warmth and student orientation projected on the above items, these same teachers endorsed taking neatness into account in grading, concern about discipline, the use of ability grouping, and avoidance of slang. While not directly contradictory, these items do not fit well with the picture presented in the items listed above.

Also, as will be explained in more detail in later chapters, self report data on items dealing with classroom practices were not always borne out by classroom observations. For example, these teachers strongly endorsed both the use of praise and the use of peer tutoring, but neither of these were observed very often by the classroom observers. Also, they taught directly rather than indirectly much more than

than they probably realized (a commonly reported finding).

The items which were unanimously or near-unanimously endorsed by the low SES teachers also included several that suggest social desirability (gaining satisfaction from working with books and ideas, small group discussions are important, let the students learn by themselves if they can, use advance organizers, allow students to choose assignments, encourage students to believe that they can succeed, use praise, spend extra time with the students if necessary). However, the responses of the low SES teachers contained a larger number of surprises, including many which make sense when one considers the kinds of students that they were teaching.

These teachers as a group were secure enough in their experiences with low SES children to strongly endorse numerous items that other teachers were less certain about, including many that did not have any clear social desirability bias (stress on knowing how to diagnose learning problems and on the importance of evaluating and recording information about students, on the importance of teacher-made tests as opposed to standardized tests, on the need for time to think and relax, agreement that facts come before generalizations, agreement that it is important to show the students the purpose of assignments, agreement that textbooks are storehouses of facts, awareness that students need to be reminded to ask when they don't understand, and endorsement of the idea that promotion should not be based on achievement alone).

The responses of these teachers indicate that they have a less romanticized view of teaching and children than do the teachers working in high SES schools. They are more concerned with how to deal with frustrations and failures than with the provision of enrichment experiences, and their responses clearly convey the impression that teaching is hard and demanding work, even though they enjoy it.

Additional information of this sort is provided by Figure 2-2 (on page 31) which shows the items that all or almost all of the teachers in the whole sample or in one of the two SES subgroups disagreed with. There were 37 of these items, some of which seem to contradict the answers to the items listed in Figure 2-1. For example, most teachers did not favor the concept of social promotion. Nevertheless, the data in Figure 2-1 revealed that teachers in low SES schools endorsed an item stating that they disagreed that non-achievers should be failed. It is possible that the wording of the latter item might have confused these teachers, so that they thought they were saying that non-achievers should be failed rather than the opposite. It is also possible, if the answers are taken at the face value, that the teachers were responding to the two items with two different sets. Their answers to the social promotion item probably reflected only the question of whether or not a child who did not master the content of the grade should be promoted to the next grade at the end of the year. In contrast, the term "should be failed" on the other item might have been responded to more in terms of everyday grading and report card grading, rather than "failed" in the sense of retention in the grade.

In any case, most of the teachers in both SES groups were against the social promotion concept, despite the lopsided research literature favoring it. In our experience, this makes these teachers typical. We find that teachers in general are against the social promotion concept even though almost all studies of the matter reveal that socially promoted students end up achieving at higher levels than students retained one or more times in a grade.

The next item also showed a difference by school SES. The high SES teachers stated that they took neatness into account in grading, but the low SES teachers stated that they did not. This is consistent with the general trend of SES differences mentioned previously.

Items showing disagreement by almost all or all teachers revealed the following. Washrooms were usually located inside the classroom; teachers tended to mark absentees but not to officially call the whole roll; seatwork correction tended to be done in interaction with the students rather than outside of class or while the students were doing something else; teachers did not believe that it was a good idea to aim instruction toward the low achievers in the room; most teachers required the students to stay on and within lines for all assignments, not just those for printing and writing; they felt that grading was relatively unimportant; they did think that it was important to emphasize a new concept when introducing it; they also thought it was important for students to discuss work among themselves; they disagreed with the idea that promotion should be based solely on academic achievement (even though they also disagreed with the idea of social promotion!); they realized that they could not require the same amount of work from all students; they realized that some deviation from the curriculum would be inevitable; they felt that clarification time was important and necessary; they saw no reason to make students stand while reciting; they felt that relevance would help develop student interest; they did not believe that much teacher talk implied good teaching; and they rejected the idea that almost all students should acquire the same knowledge and skills at the same time. For the most part, this list represents a rejection of out-dated or overly extreme ideas about school and teaching. Most of the items are self explanatory and make immediate common sense.

The biggest contradiction is in the area of social promotion. Many teachers rejected both social promotion and promotion solely on the basis of academic achievement, responses which at least at first appear contradictory. To a degree, they probably are contradictory, most probably because the term "social promotion" turns off most teachers. Despite this, the same teachers usually realized that academic achievement alone should not be the sole criterion for promotion. The teachers apparently preferred something in between. Perhaps they would have endorsed an item like "In questionable or borderline cases, a student should be promoted to the next grade, but students who clearly have not mastered the material at their grade level should be retained."

Comparisons of the differences in items that high SES vs. low SES teachers disagreed with revealed differences in teacher perceptions and role definitions, and resulting differences in the kinds of problems that the teachers thought about and considered important. The high SES teachers were against assigning large amounts of homework; against having students trade papers to grade them; unconcerned about the wide range of student achievement as a serious problem; did not think that textbooks were particularly important or crucial; did not think that teaching should be evaluated independently of student learning; believed that oral evaluation and feedback to students was important; and believed that it was better to err on the side of over-explaining than on the side of under-explaining. Most of these items are aspects of a fact that will be discussed in more detail in Chapter 3: high SES teachers were concerned primarily with putting across curriculum content and seeing that the children progressed satisfactorily.

Items that produced general disagreement among teachers in low SES schools revealed the following. These teachers were against taking neatness into account in grading assignments; believed that it was important to teach skills and facts as well as principles; believed that the material had to be interesting to the students in order to be of any real value to them; believed that it was important to call attention to mistakes and to provide feedback to the student, even if this meant interruptions; believed that visual aids were useful and important teaching tools; rejected the idea that routine would affect learning adversely; believed that affectionateness toward the children was an integral part of good teaching; believed that it was necessary to know each individual student well; did not think it was particularly important to have students repeat grammatical constructions until they got them correct; and stressed that praise was important to stimulate achievement, both in the individual student being praised and in other members of the class.

Here again, the low SES teachers differed from the high SES teachers primarily in the degree to which they presented teaching as a difficult and demanding job. The high SES teachers' responses sometimes gave the impression that they have few if any problems, and that they believed that a competent teacher will succeed with most students in the typical situation. In contrast, the responses of the low SES teachers revealed concern about student failure, concern about generating student interest in the material, concern about getting to know the students closely and providing affectionateness and other personal responses (not just giving praise for academic work), and related concerns showing that these teachers saw success in getting students to master the material as something that they had to work hard for, not something that comes more or less automatically if they do a competent job.

It is our impression that these SES setting differences in teacher responses generally reflect reality, particularly those dealing with the general issue of the difficulty of meeting teaching goals. Teachers working in high SES schools generally had relatively few serious learning or behavior problems, so that they had more time to deal with them and also more time to concern themselves with enrichment and other matters that low SES teachers would look upon as frills. Meanwhile, low SES teachers were struggling continually to find ways to get most of their students to master even the basic material. In many cases, they had to struggle just to establish a workable relationship with the students.

Consequently, seeing students achieve even minimal mastery of the content of the grade level was a rewarding gratification for these teachers, while seeing students move past basic mastery into enrichment activities, high level individualized projects, or other advanced activities consti- tuted a luxury from their point of view. In general, the low SES teachers were not complaining about all of this; they merely were stating the facts. Most of them accepted the situation and worked at making the best of it, adjusting their goals and expectations, as well as their sources of gratification and feelings of success, to more modest levels than those open to the teachers working in high SES schools.

In summary, the data in Figures 2-1 and 2-2 indicate that the teachers in the sample agreed and disagreed with a large number of items with which almost any group of teachers would be expected to agree or disagree. However, there were certain pattern differences related to the SES levels of the schools at which the teachers were working that made systematic differences in their responses. In general, teachers working in high SES schools were somewhat more conservative, were more homogeneous in their ideology (indirect teaching and discovery learning being the main themes), and seemed to take it for granted that the vast majority of students would master the material at at least satisfactory levels.

In contrast, the low SES teachers tended to picture

teaching as a difficult and demanding job, to show concern about being able to reach students emotionally and to get them to be able to master the minimum requirements of the grade, and to be concerned with generating student interest through varieties of teaching techniques, use of media, and whatever else they could find and use. In general, we believe that these SES differences in teacher statements reflected real differences in the nature of the students and the teaching tasks facing the teachers in their respective settings.

Differences Between Sample and Comparison Group Teachers

The 56 items which showed differences significant beyond the .05 level between the 30 teachers in the sample and the 38 randomly selected second and third grade teachers not in the sample are shown in Figure 2-3 (on page 33). The items cover a broad range of teaching philosophies and practices, and, with one exception, do not seem to cluster together in any obvious way. This impression gathered from simple inspection of the variables listed in Figure 2-3 was confirmed by a factor analysis of the items, which yielded only one clear cut factor of any significance. Thus, except for the items on this factor (to be discussed below), the teachers in the sample differed from other teachers at the same grades who were selected randomly on more items than would be expected by chance, but these items did not cluster together into factors and the group differences did not show clear cut, patterned differences on major variables.

The exception to this was a cluster of 10 items that formed a clear cut factor. These items were: teachers insist that students stay in place and work; teachers rigidly follow a planned schedule; teachers require that students stand while reciting; teachers feel that materials other than texts are unimportant; teachers believe that low grades reinforce effort by making students work harder to improve; teachers believe that they should spend more time talking to the whole class rather than to individuals; teachers believe that they should urge students to do better work; teachers state that the proper strategy after getting a wrong answer is to ask another student for the answer; teachers believe that they should require more from their abler students; and teachers feel that it is their responsibility to see that the students have supplies at their desks. We have labeled this combination of items the "traditionalism" factor.

On each of the ten items, and, of course, for the factor as a whole, the teachers in the sample were more likely to agree (or less likely to disagree as strongly) when compared to the teachers not in the sample. Thus, the teachers in the sample were more traditional in their beliefs and attitudes about teaching.

We were not at all surprised by this finding, because we already knew that the teachers in the sample were significantly older than the teachers not in the sample, and group comparisons of adults of different ages usually show the older groups to be more traditional in their attitudes and beliefs than the younger groups, regardless of the topics being investigated. Consequently, our first reaction to this finding was to chalk up the difference in traditionalism to the age difference between the groups, and not to anything related to consistency in producing student learning gains. In fact, we initially took the findings from these analyses as confirmation of our assumption that there would be nothing particularly unique about the teachers in the sample other than their greater than average ages and years of teaching experience.

Just to be sure, however, we conducted a second set of analyses in which teachers in the sample were compared with non-sample teachers matched as closely as possible for age and years of teaching experience. This time, as expected, the number of items showing a group difference at or beyond the .05 level of significance was reduced to 33, only eight above the 25 to be expected by chance. This seemed to provide more confirmation of the interpretation that the traditionalism factor was essentially an age factor and not something related to the consistency of the teachers in the sample in producing student learning gains. However, a factor analysis of these 33 items revealed a traditionalism factor very similar to the one listed above. Nevertheless, age still looked like the explanation, because even though the youngest and least experienced teachers had been removed from the comparison group, the sample teachers still had an average of almost ten years more teaching experience than the teachers in the comparison group. Even so, these findings had produced enough nagging doubts by this time that we decided to conduct different kinds of analyses in order to try to establish more clearly whether or not age differences explained this traditionalism factor.

These new analyses involved dividing both the sample teachers and the teachers in the comparison group into quartiles (fourths) on the basis of their number of years of teaching experience. When this was done, the average score on the traditionalism factor was computed for each quartile of teachers in each of the two groups. We expected that these analyses would reveal a simple linear relationship between traditionalism and age in both teacher groups, with the least experienced teachers showing the lowest scores and the most experienced teachers the highest scores. Much to our surprise, there was absolutely no relationship, not even a hint of a relationship, between years of teaching experience and degree of traditionalism. This was true both for teachers in the sample and for teachers in the comparison group. In short, years of teaching experience (and, in effect, teacher age) had nothing to do with degree of traditionalism in beliefs and attitudes about teaching.

We also correlated the traditionalism scores with student learning scores, to see if traditionalism in beliefs and attitudes related in any systematic way to success in producing student learning gains. These analyses revealed no significant relationships among teachers working in high SES schools, but two of the five correlations were significant for teachers working in low SES schools. For these teachers, traditionalism correlated *negatively* with student learning gains in language arts, although it was unrelated to student learning gains in arithmetic.

Considering the beliefs and attitudes that make up the traditionalism factor, its negative relationships to learning gains, particularly in view of the fact that they occurred among low SES teachers, were not surprising. Teachers with these kinds of traditional beliefs and attitudes would be expected to have difficulty teaching in low SES schools, and both these findings and many others to be discussed in subsequent chapters revealed that they did have difficulty. The really surprising thing about the traditionalism factor was not its relationships to learning gains, but its relationship to consistency, particularly in view of the fact that this relationship is not explainable on the basis of differences in teachers' ages.

It should be kept in mind that the teachers were selected for the study *solely on the basis of consistency, and not on the basis of degree of effectiveness.* Thus, the sample was *not* composed of teachers who were either highly effective or highly ineffective. We could not have selected a sample of this sort even if we had wanted to, because it happened that effectiveness levels among the consistent teachers were normally distributed. That is, the effectiveness scores of the consistent teachers were clustered mostly around the average score, with relatively few showing either very low or very high scores (see Figure 2).

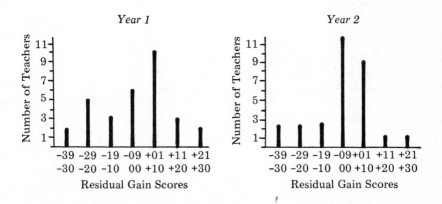

FIGURE 2. Distributions for both years of mean residual gain scores on standardized achievement tests for sample teachers (averaged across four years).

This was precisely the kind of distribution we had been hoping for, because we wanted to select for study teachers at all levels of effectiveness and to correlate their effectiveness scores with other measures (rather than to study two groups of highly effective and highly ineffective teachers and look for group differences). As Soar (1972) has pointed out, using this group difference method (selecting only teachers high and low in effectiveness) would cause investigators to miss certain important relationships between teacher behavior and student outcomes. This would occur whenever relationships were curvilinear (so that the most effective teachers had some medium amount of the teacher behavior of interest, while the less effective teachers had either too much or too little of it).

Simple group comparisons between highly effective and highly ineffective teachers would not reveal any differences on such behaviors. This is because both the highly effective group and the highly ineffective group would likely contain some teachers who were very low on the behavior and others who were very high on it. These differences within each group would cancel each other out, so that the average scores for the two groups would be similar. This would create the false impression that the teacher behavior was unrelated to effectiveness.

In contrast, when teachers are selected from the entire range of effectiveness (as we did), and when curve fitting analyses such as those used in the present study are used to analyze the data, such relationships are revealed. Because of these considerations, we selected teachers on the basis of consistency alone. Our intention was to try to get a reasonably normal distribution in degree of effectiveness, rather than to select a group of high effective teachers and a group of low effective teachers. As it turned out, selecting teachers on the basis of consistency alone yielded a sample of teachers that already was normally distributed in their effectiveness scores, so that nothing had to be done to adjust the sample.

Thus, the teachers selected for the study actually were selected on only two criteria: a minimum number of consecutive years of teaching at their grade level, and a high degree of consistency in their relative success in producing student learning gains. In theory, then, teachers included in the sample differed from other teachers with equal experience working at their grade level solely by virtue of being more consistent in their relative success in producing student learning gains (that is, solely in their *consistency* of effectiveness, not in their *degree* of effectiveness).

Given all of this, we did not expect any differences between teachers in the sample and those in the comparison group other than differences directly related to age. Therefore, we were and still are very much surprised by the findings that the teachers in the sample were more traditional in their beliefs and attitudes about teaching than the teachers in the comparison group, and that this difference is unrelated to teacher age. Apparently, there is something about more traditional teachers that makes them more likely to be consistent in their relative success in producing student learning gains, as compared with less traditional teachers.

Perhaps these two associated characteristics (traditional attitudes and consistency in producing student learning gains) are part of a more general pattern of a greater stability and resistance to change, both in beliefs and attitudes and in behavior, among the consistent and traditional teachers. In any case, the traditionalism factor described a clear difference between the teachers in the sample and those in the comparison group, and this difference was clearly related to consistency in producing student learning gains and unrelated to teacher age. We remain surprised by this finding and unable to offer any clear explanation for it. It remains as somewhat of a mystery, and also as a reminder that *consistency* in producing student learning gains probably is related to a number of other personal characteristics, independently of *degree of success* in producing student learning gains. That is, teachers who are notably consistent, regardless of their relative effectiveness, appear to have certain characteristics in common with one another that differentiate them from inconsistent teachers. Obviously, more information is needed about this, because of its many implications for pre-service and in-service teacher education.

FIGURE 2-1. Questionnaire items which showed little variance because all teachers (either in the sample as a whole or in one of the two SES subgroups) tended to agree with them.

High and Low SES (Total)

Agreement with the item:

Dressing up a lesson to make it more interesting.
Believe success is indicated by students enjoying school.
Prepare by using both unit and lesson plans.
Aim instruction to middle achievers.
Always conscious of voice quality.
Use both individual and group competition.

Best way to include parents:

In PTA and projects.
Provide warm positive home atmosphere.

Necessary to good teaching:

Patience.
Knowledge of subject matter.

Important for deciding about students:

Observations about student.

Important to teaching

Use pointer with blackboard.
Use difficult words to help students learn them.
Giving right answers is less effective than guidance in problem solving.
Encourage students to disagree with teacher's statements.
Problem solving one of main purposes of school.
Good teacher avoids doing student's work for him.
Some review everyday is good.
Impact of the teacher is far more important than the rest of the school environment.
Teaching should proceed on the principle that intellectual learning is pleasurable.
Teacher should check to see if her explanation has left some students puzzled.
Maximum learning occurs when both teacher and student

have a definite idea of what is to be done.
One should teach students how to learn effectively.

High SES Only

Agreement with the item:
  Allowing students to call out comments.
  Taking neatness into account.
  Found satisfactory rapport with students.
  Regularly uses praise as motivational technique.

Best way to include parents:
  Cooperate with school in disciplining child at home.
  Provide enriching materials at home.

Necessary to good teaching:
  Engage in peer tutoring.

Important to teaching:
  Learning by memorization may deter problem solving.
  Explanation should be short to retain interest.
  Teacher should ask frequently if students understand.
  Directive teaching produces more passive students.
  In most classes, students should be ability grouped.
  Teacher should avoid the use of slang.
  Lecture method is seldom desirable.

Low SES Only

Necessary to good teaching:
  Diagnose learning problems.
  Evaluate, record, and report.

Gain satisfaction from:
  Working with books and ideas.
  Salary and benefits.

Important for deciding about students:
  Teacher made tests.

Need more time to:
  Relax and think.

Important to teaching:
  Facts come before generalizations.

Good teacher admits ignorance openly.
Small group discussions are important.
Tell or explain nothing that students can get alone.
Advance organizers are important.
Allow students to choose assignments.
Encourage students to believe they can succeed.
Show students purpose of work.
Praise, in some way, all students' work.
A good text is a storehouse of facts.
Remind students to ask when they don't understand.
Teacher should be expected to spend some free time with
   students if it will help them learn.
Teaching is an art not a science.
Disagree that non-achievers should be failed.

Figure 2-2. Disagreements with questionnaire items.

High and Low SES (Total)

Favors social promotion.

Washroom located outside classroom.

Calls roll all year instead of just marking absentees.

Corrects seatwork by:
   Having teacher aide do it.
   Doing it herself
   Having high achievers do it.

Aim instruction to low achievers.

Require students to stay on lines only for printing and
   writing assignments.

Important to teaching:
   Grading is one of the most important functions of a teacher.
   It is not necessary to repeat or rephrase when introducing
      a new concept.
   It is a waste of time for students to discuss work among
      themselves.
   Promotion should be based on academic achievement.
   Require the same amount of work from all students.
   Don't allow deviation from instruction.
   A good teacher needs to spend little time on clarifica-
      tion.
   Students should stand while reciting.
   Relevancy will not help the disinterested student.
   Good teaching implies much teacher talk.
   All except the exceptional student should acquire same
      knowledge and skill at the same time.

High SES Only

Assigns a large amount of homework.

Corrects seatwork by:
   Having students trade papers.

Considers the following serious teacher problems:
   Wide range of student achievement.

Important to teaching:

Effective learning comes from a logically organized text.

Teaching should be evaluated independently of learning results.

One should not do a lot of oral evaluation of student's work.

Better to err in underexplaining than in overexplaining.

Low SES Only

Takes neatness into account in grading.

Important to teaching:

Only important thing to teach is a principle.

Assign material then assure students work.

Kids should master material whether or not it is interesting.

Ignore mistakes to avoid interruptions.

Most visual aids are not as good as the printed word.

Routine can adversely affect learning.

Good teaching and general affection are separate.

In an average classroom of 20+ it is unnecessary to know each student well.

Student should repeat grammar construction until correct.

Praising others does little to stimulate achievement.

Figure 2-3. Variables which discriminated between teachers in the sample and teachers in the comparison group from a 495-item questionnaire.

Descriptions	Direction[1]	Probability[2]
1. % Reading group reading, silent reading	sample +	*
2. % Reading group reading, individual reading	comparison +	*

Checklists:

3. Effect of low grades is to encourage	sample +	*
4. "Dress up" lesson to make it more interesting	comparison +	*
5. Measure of success: children get down to work	sample +	*
6. Preparation: all subjects within units	sample +	**
7. Writing requirements	comparison +	*
8. Amount of different assignments on any given day	comparison +	*

Motivation Techniques:

9. Smiling faces, gold stars, etc.	comparison +	*
10. Contests, competitive games	comparison +	*
11. Individual prizes, rewards	sample +	*

Beliefs About Good Teaching:

12. Clarify attitudes, beliefs, problems	sample +	*
13. Participate in professional and civic life	sample +	**

Descriptions	Direction[1]	Probability[2]
14. Allow students to become involved in ugly or distressing aspects of subjects	comparison +	*
15. Require undivided attention	sample +	**
16. Insist students stay in place and work	sample +	**
17. Focus attention on student's work and ideas vs. teacher's	comparison +	*
18. After wrong answer, ask another	sample +	**
19. Rigidly follow planned schedule	sample +	**
20. Provide an exact model for student's work	sample +	**
21. Patience	comparison +	*
22. Knowledge of subject matter	sample +	*
23. Uses slang with children	comparison +	*
24. See that students have supplies at desk	sample +	**
25. Knowledge and use of behavior modification techniques	comparison +	*

Satisfactions in Teaching:

26. Working with books and ideas	sample +	**
27. Working with principal and supervisors	sample +	**
28. Planning lessons	sample +	*

NEA Teacher Problem Survey:

29. More authority to develop inservice programs	comparison +	*

Descriptions	Direction[1]	Probability[2]
Educational Opinion Inventory:		
30. Material besides texts is unimportant	sample +	*
31. Education should teach people what to think	sample +	*
32. Teacher should teach the prescribed course without deviation	sample +	*
33. Students should be told that they can get their school work if they really try	sample +	**
34. Strong emphasis should be placed on mastery of subject matter and memorization of facts	sample +	*
35. Students should not all be encouraged to attack schoolwork in the same way	comparison +	*
36. Require more of abler students	sample +	**
37. Memory assignments should be frequent	sample +	**
38. Require same amount of work from all	sample +	*
39. Students should be required to stand when reciting	sample +	**
40. Most visual aids aren't as good as the printed word	sample +	**
41. Effective learning comes from logically organized textbook	sample +	*
42. Teacher should continue to urge a student to do better work	sample +	*

Descriptions	Direction[1]	Probability[1]
43. Last 3—4 days— where summary and integration go on— can make a semester succeed or fail	comparison +	*
44. Impact of teacher is far more important than all other aspects of the school environment combined	sample +	*
45. Teachers should use some of the students' own "lingo" or slang	comparison +	**
46. Key to learning is high standards and pressure	sample +	**
47. Failure is most often due to laziness	sample +	*
48. In an average classroom of 20+, it's unnecessary to know individual students well	sample +	*
49. Insight into nature of number system will not reduce amount of drill necessary in teaching math	sample +	**
50. Teacher should look more to the class as a whole when talking, rather than at individual students	sample +	**
51. All except the exceptional students should acquire the same knowledge and skills at about the same time	sample +	*
52. The lecture method is seldom desirable	comparison +	*

Descriptions	Direction[1]	Probability[1]
53. Teachers lose effectiveness because they are so energetic	sample +	*

Teacher Concerns Checklist: (I am concerned about . . .)

54. Rapid rate of curriculum and instructional change	sample +	**
55. The values and attitudes of the current generation	sample +	*

Career Information:

56. MA or MEd degree Yes 1 No 2	sample +	**

---

[1]The direction indicates which of the two groups had the higher mean.
[2]Probability values are: $p < .05$ shown by one asterisk and $p < .01$ shown by two asterisks.

Teacher Attitudes and Role Definitions

3

We begin our discussion of the correlates of teaching effectiveness with a cluster of variables describing the attitudes and beliefs that teachers bring into the classroom with them. These variables, measured through interview and questionnaire techniques, are called *presage* variables. This is to distinguish them from *process* variables, which refer to the observed teacher-student interaction which occurs in the classroom. Presage variables include general aspects of teacher personality as well as certain specific beliefs and attitudes.

Perhaps the most pervasive and fundamental presage variable which appeared in our study was the teacher's basic role definition. Some teachers perceived the job of teaching as an interesting and worthwhile challenge, approached it with resourcefulness and dedication, and took personal

responsibility for the learning of their students. They perceived plenty of problems, all right, but they also believed
that they were capable of overcoming these problems.
In contrast, the less successful teachers were more likely
to look upon teaching as "just a job," and to respond to
problems and frustrations by giving up and attributing failure to outside causes. Instead of redoubling their efforts
and searching for ways to solve problems, they tended to
rationalize their failures in ways that allowed them to avoid
assuming personal responsibility, and to discuss the problems
as if they were simply too serious to be solvable. They
couldn't teach very successfully because they had too many
students, because the range of student ability in their classrooms was too great, because they lacked the appropriate
materials, because they didn't have enough help, because
the students themselves and/or their parents didn't care,
etc.

It is important to note that the difference between
successful and unsuccessful teachers was not in the presence
or absence of these problems themselves, but in the ways
that the teachers reacted to them. Successful teachers had
the same kinds of problems, but they responded with behavior designed to overcome them, not with resignation
and defeat. Thus, a fundamental attribute of the successful
teachers was a "can do" attitude, a feeling that they were
capable of coping with whatever problems came along.
Coupled with this was the assumption of personal responsibility for whatever might happen in the classroom. These
teachers felt that they could and would control what happened in the classroom, and consequently they attributed
responsibility for what happend to themselves. In contrast,
teachers who felt powerless to cope with problems usually
attempted to shift responsibility to factors outside of their
control (administrative and structural restrictions, attitudes
of the students or their families, etc.). The successful teachers
did not always succeed, of course, but their determined
attitude probably helped them to succeed appreciably more
often in given situations than teachers who were convinced
that they couldn't handle the problems (and thus didn't
even try, or tried only halfheartedly).

This complex of attitudes and beliefs appears to be a special case of the more general psychological variable of **locus of control.** Locus of control is a basic personality dimension that has been found to correlate with achievement striving, persistence, seeking success versus trying to avoid failure, and taking personal responsibility for outcomes (versus feeling that one cannot control one's environment or the outcomes of one's behavior). To the extent that the locus of control over the outcomes of one's actions is perceived as *internal,* that is, within the person, one is likely to believe that he is responsible for his successes and failures and that he can change things, at least to some degree.

In contrast, to the extent that the locus of control over outcomes is presumed to be external to the person and beyond his control, he will tend to believe that what happens to him is largely a matter of fate, luck, or other forces that are larger than he is and are beyond his control. When faced with frustrations or problems, the person who feels a sense of personal control is more likely to strive to overcome the problems and to feel that he will be likely to succeed. In contrast, the person who doesn't feel that he has this kind of control is unlikely to strive (What difference would it make?), and consequently is more likely to rationalize failures by pointing out that there was nothing he could do anyway, because of various forces which prevented him from succeeding.

This fundamental belief in the degree to which one can control the outcomes of one's actions appears to be an important determinant of achievement behavior (striving to reach goals), particularly behavior in challenging or threatening situations. Our data suggest that this is just as true in the classroom in respect to the challenges faced by the teacher as it is in other aspects of life. Thus, other things being equal, the teacher who feels capable of handling problems is likely to assume personal responsibility for handling them and to take action which is likely to succeed in solving them. Conversely, the teacher who doesn't feel this sense of control is likely to evade responsibility and not even try to make a serious attempt to solve the problem.

Who's In Charge?

Teacher differences in locus of control showed up in other attitudes and also in their behavior in the classroom. Teachers who felt a sense of inner control and took personal responsibility for what went on in their classrooms showed that *they were in charge.* They designed and maintained the general learning environment of the classroom. Although they often solicited or accepted suggestions from the children, they retained control over what went on, how it went on, and when it went on. These teachers also tended to be the ones who were the most successful in obtaining student learning gains.

In contrast, the classrooms of other teachers presented a picture of chaos (in a few cases), or more typically, of a certain degree of disorder due to the absence of planning, control, and even goals, long or short range. A much greater percentage of things that went on in these classrooms was unplanned by the teacher, including a fair percentage that was not desired by the teacher. When unexpected things did come up, these teachers often appeared confused about how to respond to them. As a result, the initiative in structuring classroom interaction often was assumed and maintained by the students. Much time was wasted because the teacher was fighting for attention or control, trying to make up her mind about how to handle a situation, or to find out just what had happened. Thus, this greater degree of student initiative did not indicate greater freedom or creativity. On the contrary, it usually meant wasted time or time spent dealing with disruptions and behavior problems. In contrast, most of the time in the classrooms run by the more successful teachers was spent in worthwhile activities in which the students were continually and actively engaged.

Individualizing Instruction

Differences in teacher role definitions and attitudes showed up quite clearly in differences in how they responded to student learning problems. The more successful teachers made it their business to see that the students learned, regardless of how much time or effort this might involve. Consequently, they were doggedly persistent in working with slow students to help them overcome failure. This was especially true of the more successful teachers working in low SES schools, who not only showed these traits in their teaching behavior, but stated that they valued them in their responses to interview and questionnaire items.

Successful teachers in general spent much time seeing that slower students got the individual reteaching and extra practice that they needed. They did much of this personally, although sometimes they provided individual attention through peer tutoring or similar mechanisms. In any case, students who were having difficulty with the fundamental tool skills of reading, writing, and arithmetic received specialized practice exercises, tutorial assistance, reteaching of small amounts of new material with great redundancy to the point of overlearning, and the like. This stress on teaching to the point of overlearning was important, because research on learning has shown that skills mastered to the point of overlearning (that is, the point at which more practice doesn't yield more improvement—the person has mastered the skill to the limits of his ability) tend to remain with the person permanently.

In contrast, skills learned only partially and not to the point of overlearning tend to be lost over time, due to forgetting. Although the successful teachers were not necessarily aware of this principle in its more formal statement, they were aware of the importance of providing a child with a solid foundation in basic skills, and they included this task as part of their definition of their jobs.

Attitudes Toward Students

The successful teachers usually had quite realistic attitudes toward students and teacher-student relationships. Although they liked children and enjoyed the interpersonal aspects of teaching, they took a professionalized view of their students, looking upon them primarily as young learners with whom they interacted within a teacher-student relationship. In contrast, the less successful teachers tended to take one of two contradictory extreme overreactions to students. The more common of these was a romanticized notion of the student as a warm, wonderful, lovely, precious, etc. person who was a great pleasure just to be around. In our observations, teachers who painted this rosy picture of students were not more likely to be warm toward them or to appear to be enjoying their jobs any more than teachers with less romantic and more realistic views. In fact, a few of the more gushy teachers had highly chaotic classrooms (perhaps because they couldn't bring themselves to impose order upon the class), which occasionally became so out of control that the teacher exploded in anger and punitiveness in spite of herself. The more successful teachers also were successful classroom managers (see Chapter 4), so that such explosions seldom were necessary.

⁓There also were a few disillusioned and bitter teachers who looked upon students as "the enemy." They were usually teaching in schools that they disliked or were upset because the kind of student now coming to their school was not the kind of student that they preferred and were accustomed to. In short, these teachers were teachers who valued conformity and deference to authority by students, and they had not learned to cope with students who did not have these characteristics. Presumably they realized at some level that they had not learned how to cope, so that they rationalized their failures as teachers by blaming the students (and sometimes also their families or even their racial or ethnic group). Thus, the successful teachers tended to have balanced and realistic attitudes toward students, while the unsuccessful teachers usually had either romanticized, rosy attitudes or cynical and hostile attitudes.

⁓ These attitudes showed up in teaching process behaviors. The more successful teachers tended to speak in a calm, normal tone of voice and to concentrate most of their interactions on curriculum-related activities. In contrast, the teachers with romanticized attitudes often taught in gushy tones and spent much time cultivating their personal relationships with children and discussing personal matters having nothing to do with the curriculum. In fact, part of the reason that these teachers were relatively less successful in producing student learning gains was that they simply did not spend as much time trying to do so.

Finally, the teachers with cynical and hostile attitudes tended to "bark" at the children, and also to spend much time dealing with procedural and behavioral matters. Partly because of their own behavior, control and discipline problems were especially frequent in their classrooms (see Chapter 4), so that they featured a more or less continuing cycle of undesirable actions and reactions.

— The more successful teachers looked upon themselves as diagnosticians and problem solvers, rather than as "mother-substitutes" or disciplinarians. They enjoyed and cultivated personal relationships with the children to a degree, and they instituted and enforced classroom rules as necessary, but their primary attention was centered upon teaching the curriculum. Although they had great respect for the children's mental capacities and thirst for learning, they realized that most of the children's work at this level required careful monitoring and provision of swift and appropriate feedback. The children were not yet ready for self-guided instruction that they could carry out on their own, independently of the teachers. Consequently, these teachers maximized the time that they spent teaching the children, particularly time spent closely monitoring individual work and providing individual feedback.

In contrast, many of the less successful teachers seemed to think that it was sufficient for them merely to present material, pass out exercises, and give grades. Apparently, they either thought that the children somehow would learn "automatically" merely upon being exposed to the curriculum materials, or they were trying to use indirect teaching or discovery learning approaches which assume that the learner will take primary responsibility for learning and which relegate the teacher to a more passive, resource-person role. In any case, the more successful teachers took personal responsibility for their students' learning and spent a lot of time teaching them, whereas the less successful teachers simply presented the material and expected the students to handle it on their own from there.

Few teachers, successful or unsuccessful, gave homework at these grade levels, and the few who did usually taught at the high SES schools. This is yet another aspect of the young child's need for monitoring and feedback when he works on exercises. The teachers apparently recognized that homework would be relatively less useful than seatwork which could be corrected, so they rarely if ever assigned homework (in fact, homework could actually induce bad habits in the child, if he were to initiate and practice incorrect habits which were not corrected because the teacher was not present). The few teachers who did favor homework usually saw it primarily as a mechanism for involving the parent in the child's learning process, and not as a teaching vehicle. Consequently, they assigned mostly review exercises as homework, and their intent was primarily to get the parent interacting with the child on school related activities, not to supplement school learning time with out-of-school learning time.

Beliefs and attitudes toward minority groups (blacks and Mexican-Americans in this case) were generally unrelated to teaching effectiveness or to the race of ethnicity of the teacher. Most were related to the degree of experience that the teacher had had with the group in question. A few high SES teachers gave rather rosy pictures of black and/or Mexican-American children, but they pointed out that their responses were based upon working with a very small number of such children, and that the children that they had encountered were unusually high in the educational level and social class background of their families. *De facto* segregation in urban schools is such that the teachers in high SES schools either never had worked with a single minority group child at all or had worked with so few that they could remember them all clearly.

The responses of teachers who taught minority group children regularly were entirely different. These teachers found it meaningless and impossible to generalize about

either blacks or Mexican-Americans, because they had long
since discovered that such stereotypic generalizations do not
hold up. They had ceased to think in group terms, looking instead upon the individual student and his unique characteristics. With the exception of a very small number of dis-
gruntled teachers who had been assigned to low SES schools
against their wills and had very negative attitudes toward the
children, this stress on the uniqueness of the individual was
common to almost all teachers working in low SES schools,
regardless of their levels of effectiveness in producing student
learning gains.

There were other SES differences in teacher beliefs and
attitudes which also reflected differences in experiences
which tended to make a difference in what a teacher looked
upon as "normal." In general, teachers in high SES schools
were more "professional" in their responses to questionnaires
and interview items, giving answers more closely resembling
what is stressed in teacher education textbooks than teachers
in low SES schools gave. The high SES teachers were more
likely to have a particular theoretical position regarding
teaching, and more likely to stress matters of curriculum and
instruction than matters related to student needs or individual differences. In contrast, low SES teachers tended to have
an attitude of, "If one method doesn't work, keep trying
until you find one that does." They stressed individual student needs and the importance of finding a way to reach the
student, and they were not particularly concerned with
theoretical issues.

Another SES difference was that the high SES teachers
had a definite preference for high achieving children, perhaps
because they could afford to do so. In any case, given their
choice, they would prefer to work with high achievers. They
left little room for flexibility regarding the curriculum (tending to believe that all of the children should master the same
curriculum, at a minimum). They also believed that children
who failed to master the curriculum should be flunked and
retained in the grade rather than given a social promotion.
Teachers working with low SES students, regardless of effectiveness, were less likely to hold such attitudes.

*Teachers work more closely
w/ higher achievers + you
at. others*

Self-fulfilling Prophecies

Much educational research has supported the idea that teachers' attitudes and expectations can act as self-fulfilling prophecies (Brophy and Good, 1974). That is, once a teacher develops a particular attitude or belief, she may begin to treat students differentially in ways that help bring about the outcomes that she expects. For example, a teacher who expects a child to be friendly may treat him in a warm way that causes him to respond in a friendly fashion, while a teacher who expects a child to be antisocial may treat him overly gingerly or distantly in a way that causes the child to feel rejected and to respond with indifference or hostility. Similarly, a teacher who expects high achievement from a child may communicate this to the child in ways which help him build confidence. She may also maximize his achievement by teaching him optimally, while she may treat a child for whom she hold low expectations quite differently. With the latter child, she might communicate her low expectations in ways that reduce the child's self esteem and confidence, and she might teach the child less material, rationalizing this on the grounds that he is not capable of learning certain things and that time spent trying to teach them to him would be time wasted. These are but a few examples of self-fulfilling prophecies: expectations, initially untrue or at least not necessarily true, which are made to come true through systematic behavior based on the belief that they will become true.

Much of the material discussed in this chapter is related to the self-fulfilling prophecy phenomenon. Teachers who believe that they can teach the children what they are supposed to learn tend to take responsibility for doing so and to set about getting the job done, while teachers who do not believe that they can do so tend to avoid this responsibility and to fail to fulfill it. Teachers who see themselves as capable of taking and keeping charge of classroom activities tend to be in charge, while teachers who are not so sure that they can run things tend not to be in charge.

The upshot of all this is that one fundamental aspect of teacher effectiveness is the teacher's **role definition**. How does the teacher define the teaching task? What is seen as

possible versus impossible? What is seen as part of her responsibility versus not her responsibility? What are her expectations about students and the nature of the teacher-student relationship?

The answers to these and related questions define each
teacher's role definition, and they also indicate what kinds of
things the teacher will and will not try to do. Many of these
decisions and the teaching behavior resulting from them ultimately will produce self-fulfilling prophecy effects, for the
simple reason that a teacher is much more likely to succeed
in doing something that she believes that she can do and that
she is deliberately trying to do than she is likely to achieve
something that she believes that she cannot do and is not
making an attempt to do. A teacher who has the general
belief that students will learn what they are taught is likely
to be an effective teacher, because she is likely to attempt to
teach them everything that they "should" learn.

Classroom Management

4

Of the process behaviors measured through classroom observation in our study, the group that had the strongest and most consistent relationships with student learning gains dealt with the classroom management skills of the teachers. By "classroom management," we mean planning and conducting activities in an orderly fashion; keeping students actively engaged in lessons and seatwork activities; and minimizing disruptions and discipline problems. Our approach to both the conceptualization and the measurement of teacher behavior in these areas was influenced heavily by the previous work of Kounin (1970).

Using a common sense approach to this important topic, Kounin conducted a study involving comparing video tapes of teachers who were notably successful classroom managers (their classrooms ran smoothly and "automatically") with video tapes of teachers who were notably unsuccessful (they had chaotic, strife-ridden classrooms). Initially, Kounin focused on the ways that the teachers dealt with inattention, disruption, and disobedience, seeking to find consistent differences between the two groups of teachers that would explain their differential success. Given the kinds of teachers included in the study, it seemed very likely that such differences would be found with this approach (in fact, taking into account the importance of the topic, one wonders why many such studies had not been done previously). In any case, the upshot of Kounin's initial efforts was a wash-out. He and his colleagues kept looking, but they could not find *any* systematic differences between successful and unsuccessful teachers in the ways that they coped with discipline problems.

Fortunately, however, in the process of observing the tapes, Kounin and his colleagues noted several other differences in teachers that seemed to be related to their differential success in classroom management. By conceptualizing these and developing ways to code them, they did succeed in finding strong and consistent differences between successful and unsuccessful classroom managers. The term "classroom managers" is used here in preference to a term like "disciplinarians," because of the nature of the differences that Kounin and his colleagues found. Briefly, the successful classroom managers were successful because they kept their students actively engaged in productive classroom work most of the time, thus minimizing the amount of trouble that they had to deal with. They were more successful because they reduced the frequency of trouble, not because they were more skilled at dealing with trouble when it appeared.

Finer analyses revealed *why* they were more successful in preventing trouble. First, their seatwork assignments were more interesting and varied, and more closely attuned to the ability levels of their students. Thus, their students were willing and able to work on them continuously instead of finishing them quickly and then having nothing to do, or, alternatively, being unable to get very far and giving up in frustration. Also, the successful classroom managers had classrooms that seemed to run smoothly, almost "automatically." However, analyses revealed that this apparently automatic smoothness actually resulted from the teacher's careful planning and organizing. Classroom monitor assignments were made to handle certain daily business that can cause frustrating delays and wasting of time if not handled efficiently. Things that were not taken care of through monitor assignments were done with efficiency, so that less time was spent standing around and waiting while materials were being passed out, possessions were collected in preparation for leaving the room, etc.

The successful classroom managers also had a quality that Kounin and his colleagues called **"withitness,"** a term they coined to describe the teacher who is regularly aware of and monitoring events going on in all parts of the room, regardless of what she might be doing at the moment. Such teachers were capable of spotting potentially disruptive problems in their early stages, and thus of nipping them in the bud before they spread and became more serious. In contrast, teachers who tended to get more wrapped up in what they were doing in their own particular spot in the room, so that they were less aware of what was going on elsewhere, were more likely to fail to notice something happening or to not notice it until it had become a major problem.

Related to this was what they called the "ripple effect." If one or two students began misbehaving and the teacher stopped it appropriately, the problem usually ended there. However, if the teacher didn't notice it or allowed it to go on too long, it often spread to other students and became more serious as well as more widespread. The "withit" teachers were more likely to anticipate such potential problems and respond appropriately. Also, if the teacher were to overreact by becoming angry or upset, this tended to stop the immediate problem with students who caused this reaction, but the whole class responded by becoming noticeably more tense and anxious, and the frequency of disobedience and other disiplinary problems tended to increase. Again, the "withit" teachers were more likely to handle the problem calmly and effectively and less likely to "blow up" in a way that would cause other problems to develop shortly.

These results are impressive when taken as a set. They

not only differentiate clearly between successful and unsuccessful classroom managers; they also go a long way toward explaining why the two types of teachers were so
differentially successful.

The variables discussed by Kounin and his colleagues were
measured in the present study through both low and high inference classroom observation instruments. In general, our data
provide strong support for Kounin's, indicating that the qualities associated with successful classroom management are essentially those that he and his colleagues discussed. Furthermore, as it turns out, these qualities not only were associated
with successful classroom management, but also with success in
producing student learning gains. The reasons seem obvious:
teachers who have few discipline problems therefore have most
of their time available for teaching and are more likely to
teach successfully compared to teachers who spend significant
amounts of time fighting for attention or trying to deal with
severe disruptions and discipline problems.

We also found that student engagement in lessons and
activities was the key to successful classroom management.
The successful teachers ran smooth, well placed lessons with
few interruptions, and their students worked consistently at
their seatwork. Although we did not measure the seatwork
for interest value, it was clear that the seatwork of the more
successful teachers was more individualized and more appropriate for each particular student, because the students in
these teachers' classrooms tended to work more consistently
and with fewer interruptions on their seatwork assignments.

Furthermore, teachers usually had developed "automatic" mechanisms to provide the students with help if they
needed it. Usually, one or more students was designated as
the person to whom a fellow student could go to for help if
he were unclear about an assignment. The assignments were
usually written on the board or displayed in some standard
place where the student could go to to double check if he
were unsure about what to do. Certain times were established
for students to come to the teacher for help, and at other
times the teacher would systematically go around the room
and check work.

All of these factors in combination tended to insure

that: *(a)* each student knew what his assignment was; *(b)* if he needed help, he could get it from the teacher or from some designated person; *(c)* he was accountable for completing the assignment appropriately because he knew that his work would be checked; *(d)* all of this was accomplished within a system of regulations that on the one hand made it possible for students who needed help to get it but at the same time made it possible for the teacher to concentrate on reading groups without being continually interrupted by students who wanted to ask questions about seatwork.

Finally, the successful classroom managers usually also had a system set up so that students knew what to do when they finished an assignment. Usually, they could choose from among various options (read, go to various learning centers, play with available games, etc.). The main points were that specific options were provided and that students knew that certain things were acceptable and certain other things were not acceptable (particularly not causing disruption or unnecessarily interrupting the teacher at times when she was busy with a reading group).

In contrast to the above, the less successful classroom managers apparently did not have their seatwork assignments well matched to their students' needs, because students finishing very quickly and then having nothing to do and/or students giving up in frustration were common. When students did come to the teacher for help, they often disrupted the teacher from conducting a lesson, because the teacher had not set up mechanisms to regulate when and how students should come to them for help. When they finished a seatwork assignment (or just stopped working on it), the students sometimes created disruptions, because the teacher had not set out clear alternatives concerning behavioral options at such times. In short, the unsuccessful classroom managers had not done the necessary preparation of individualized assignments and spare time activities, nor had they established an effective set of regulations about what students should do when they needed help with an assignment or when they had finished an assignment and did not have anything else to do.

Other factors also were involved in making certain

teachers more "withit" than others. Some of these were sheer physical layout factors. The most successful teachers usually taught small groups (usually reading groups) while stationed so that they could monitor events going on elsewhere in the classroom. In contrast, the less successful teachers often positioned themselves so that they could not easily monitor the entire classroom.

Another aspect of "withitness" was the teachers' apparent awareness of the importance of **monitoring** what was going on in the classroom. Some teachers got so caught up in the immediate aspects of what they were doing that they failed to monitor what was going on elsewhere until forced to do so by a disruptive problem. Also, the more effective teachers moved around the room regularly, sometimes to check seatwork and at other times simply to move around. Even when they were not physically moving, they visually scanned the classroom regularly to keep continual track of what was going on. Since the likelihood of children acting out disruptively seemed to be highly correlated with the likelihood of not being seen by the teacher, the more "withit" teachers had many fewer disruptions started by a child who thought that he could get away with something because the teacher wouldn't see him.

Our data also provided much support for Kounin's comments concerning ripple effects. The more "withit" teachers were more likely to prevent the spread of a problem by handling it through some appropriate intervention before it became serious. Also, when they did have to intervene, they tended to avoid the kind of strong negative reactions which Kounin had found to produce anxiety and tension (and, ultimately, a higher frequency of misbehavior). Thus, instead of lashing out at the offending child with punishment, criticism, or some other intense reaction, the more effective teachers confined their responses to simple warnings. They served notice on the relevant children that their behavior had to change, but they did so in a calm and controlled manner.

Even so, they were extremely vigilant. The more successful teachers made few target errors (blaming the wrong child) or timing errors (waiting too long to intervene, so that a minor problem became a major one), two of the major mistakes noted by Kounin in his observations of poor classroom managers. However, the more successful teachers were coded more often by the observers for "overreacting," meaning that the observers thought that the teacher reacted more strongly than the situation called for. This was especially likely to be positively associated with learning gains in the low SES schools, where disruption was a greater and more frequent problem. This finding relates to the point made in the previous chapter: the more successful teachers took and kept charge of their classrooms, refusing to be conditioned by the children.

The finding concerning ratings of overreactions seems at first to conflict with Kounin's findings concerning ripple effects following strong negative teacher reactions. However, it needs to be taken in the general context of our findings concerning teacher reactions to control problems. First, overreactions were infrequent. Successful classroom managers were much more likely to be coded for having made no errors at all than for having made a timing error, a target error, or an overreaction. When they were coded for an error, however, the error was more likely to be an overreaction than one of the other two types. Thus, these teachers were more vigilant and quicker to intervene than the less effective classroom managers, who were more likely to make timing or target errors.

Also, it should be kept in mind that, despite the ratings for overreactions, these same teachers also had a greater proportion of warnings to criticisms, suggesting that the "overreactions" coded by the classroom observers were not intensely strong negative reactions. In short, the data as a whole showed quite clearly that these teachers were particularly vigilant but not particularly critical or negativistic in their response to the students. In fact, in low SES schools especially, they were relatively warmer and more affectionate toward the children than the less successful teachers. At the same time, however, they did not tolerate disobedience.

Smoothness showed up in the "automatic" ways that these classrooms operated because of well thought out monitor systems. This was especially obvious during transitional periods between activities. In well organized classrooms, transitions lasted only a short time and the children seemed to go about shifting from one activity to another "automatically." In contrast, transitional periods in less well organized classrooms tended to be chaotic, with children wandering around, bumping into one another, confused, needing to ask the teacher what to do, etc. The teacher often was harried during these times, shouting out orders and attempting to do 10 or 15 things at the same time. Also, this type of unstructured shifting fostered pushing and shoving, thus setting the stage for fights or other more serious control problems. The more well organized teachers, in contrast, had all of these things under control because they had developed mechanisms, primarily the use of student monitors, to handle these situations more or less automatically as they came up.

This was accomplished, in addition to the use of well planned monitoring systems, by using a good set of **classroom rules.** The well organized teachers had relatively few classroom rules. These rules were fairly general, having to do with general standards of behavior (attention, respect for the teacher and for classmates, walking quietly rather than running or making noise, etc.), and they tended to be fairly flexible, so that the teacher could interpret them strictly or loosely depending upon the immediate situation. Probably most importantly, the rules were very well explained at the beginning of the year. According to the teachers, this was done in a session which the teacher either expounded the rules to the children and participated with them in a quasi-democratic rule making session.

In either case, the more successful teachers took pains to explain both the rule itself and the reason behind it to the children. This was important in helping the children to see the need for the rule and, therefore, to accept it. It also was important for its sheer information value (many children would not have been able to understand the reason for a rule if it was not explained to them). In contrast to this middle of the road system with good explanations and built-in flexibility, the less well organized and successful teachers tended to have either no rules at all (so that they were continually making *ad hoc* decisions that distracted them from teaching tasks), or else to have so many rules that the rules became overly specific and essentially meaningless. Also, they tended not to explain their rules sufficiently, so that the children could not see the logic underlying them and could not be expected to be motivated to follow them on their own.

SES Differences

Although the same basic general principles of classroom management were important in both low and high SES classrooms, there were some differences in what was optimal. The high SES children, on the average, were more capable of assuming independent responsibility, moving freely about the classroom, exercising some choice among assignments, and working independently or in cooperative small groups. Consequently, the more successful teachers working in high SES schools tended to allow the children these privileges and opportunities to the extent that they were able to handle them and benefit from them. In contrast, most low SES children were not yet ready for this kind of independent responsibility, and they usually needed more restrictions on movement about the classroom and more structure concerning assignments. Consequently, the more successful low SES school teachers were more restrictive and provided more structure.

In low SES classrooms, it was especially important for the teacher to be ready, willing, and able to deal with serious problems, since serious problems were much more likely here than in high SES schools. The successful teachers usually dealt with them, and dealt with them appropriately. In contrast, the less successful teachers either tried to avoid dealing with them altogether (such as by sending the child to the principal), or else responded with some kind of punitive overreaction that did not deal with the problem appropriately. Teachers in high SES schools did not have to deal with serious behavior problems often, if at all. The children in these classrooms still accepted adult authority without much testing or challenging. Consequently, in high SES classrooms it was more important for the teacher to provide a stimulating and interesting environment that would afford the children opportunities to do interesting and enjoyable things when they finished their assignments, while in low SES classrooms it was more important for the teachers to make sure that the children got assignments that they could handle and to make sure that the assignments were done.

In closing, it should be noted that the most appropriate method of dealing with a particular child or class varies according to the developmental level of the child or class. In particular, it should be noted that what is optimal will change to the extent that the teacher has been successful! That is, a teacher who has brought along a class (or an individual student) nicely through careful structuring eventually will get them to the point where they are ready for some independent responsibility. It is important for teachers to remain aware of this developmental trend, because what is optimal for a child who is having difficulty with initial assignments concerning tool skill mastery and who needs careful structuring and considerable encouragement is very different from what is optimal for this same child when he reaches the stage where he has mastered tool skills and has acquired the independent behavior and learning habits that make it possible for him to profit from independent and self chosen activities.

This is another reason why flexibility in rules is so important, also. The rules that are appropriate at the beginning of the year might well become decreasingly appropriate as the year goes on, and might best be replaced with a completely or partially new set of rules one or more times as the year progresses. In any case, the general point here is that classroom rules and general approaches to classroom management should be adjusted to take into account changes in the children as they occur. Different children, and even the same children at different levels of development, require different treatment for optimal results.

Matching Teaching to Student Needs and Abilities

5

In Chapter 4, we noted that continuous engagement in seatwork was one important aspect of a well organized classroom, and that matching the seatwork assignments to the interests and ability levels of the students was one key to insuring this kind of student engagement. In the present chapter, we will expand upon the more general topic of matching demands to student interests and particularly to student ability and achievement levels, this time stressing the instructional benefits more than the management benefits (although the latter still apply and remain important).

The very idea of individualizing instruction implies that there is a certain level of difficulty or content specificity that is *optimal* for each student. This idea has been propounded by writers with views as different as those of Hunt (1961) who describes "the problem of the match" (the need for teachers to match materials and assignments to the present interests and abilities of the student) and Ausubel (1963), who has pointed out that the most important determinant of student learning is the student's present level of abilities and knowledge in the subject matter area (implying that learning will proceed optimally if new input is matched to present structure). The statements of these writers, the concept of individualization, and numerous related concepts all imply a curvilinear relationship between the difficulty level of instruction and the value of the learning experience. Learning will be most optimal when presented at the optimal difficulty level. If the material is either too easy or too difficult, learning will not proceed as well.

This fundamental principle showed itself many different ways in our data. Perhaps the most obvious area was in the percentages of teacher questions which were answered correctly by the students (which in turn were related to the difficulty levels of the questions that the teachers asked). Relationships between these variables and student learning gains were curvilinear for both SES groups. High SES students learned most optimally when they answered about 70% of their teachers' questions correctly; low SES students learned most optimally when they answered about 80% of their teachers' questions correctly.

Several things are noteworthy about these findings. First, the curvilinear relationships confirm the general ideas underlying individualization, particularly the idea that there is an optimal level of difficulty which will produce more learning than material that is either easier or more difficult. Second, the SES difference in optimal levels provides an indication of the nature of the kind of individualization that is required. Since SES is a "proxy" variable which stands for a complex of ability, achievement, and motivation, extrapolation from this finding suggests that low SES children (and, by implication, less competent children of any SES level, compared to more competent children in the same class) learn more by having less taught to them, but by having it taught to them redundantly to the point of overlearning, proceeding in small steps that they can master without undue cognitive strain. In contrast, somewhat more competent children can cover the same material more quickly, and furthermore will learn more optimally by being challenged with slightly more difficult questions and assignments.

A third item worth noting concerning these findings is their bearing on the "errorless learning" hypothesis. Errorless learning advocates, who include most writers of programmed texts, assume that learning is optimal when it proceeds errorlessly. Taken literally, this would mean that learning would be optimal when the student answered 100% of questions or assignment items correctly. This assumes a linearly negative relationship between difficulty level and learning rate.

Our curvilinear data dispute this. They do indicate that learning proceeds most smoothly when the new material is *relatively easy* to assimilate (notice that the optimal levels were up around 75% of questions answered correctly, rather than down at lower levels which would indicate more difficult material). However, the percentages are still considerably different from 100%. What this means, of course, is that, although learning does proceed most smoothly when there is no undue cognitive strain, learning must also involve some new challenge and a certain amount of failure or confusion if there is going to be any forward progress at all. If we literally taught at an errorless rate, we would be continually teaching the same old material over and over again, for the most part.

While errorless learning advocates would posit a 100% success rate as optimal, social scientists concerned with achievement motivation would posit a 50% success rate as optimal. This idea is based on several laboratory experiments which have indicated that achievement motivation is strongest when the probability of succeeding is 50%. However, taking these data and attempting to apply them directly to the problem of the difficulty level of classroom material is a classic example of attempting to generalize laboratory data to naturalistic situations without taking other relevant factors into account.

First, these data have come almost exclusively from game-like experimental situations, such as horseshoes, ring

toss, and building block towers. Most of the activities involved were physical skill activities involving little or no
cognitive work. Thus, while it may be true that physical skill
activities are most enjoyable and engender the most achievement motivation when they are at about a 50% difficulty
level, it appears that cognitive activities which are at a 50%
difficulty level are too difficult and produce too much cognitive strain for most people.

Second, the data from the achievement motivation experiments concern the relationships between difficulty level
and achievement motivation, or desire to achieve, as con-
trasted with the relationships between difficulty level and
measured achievement *per se*. That is, they concern the relationship between difficulty level and the person's *desire to
achieve* on the task, not his *actual achievement* on the task.
Other studies of motivation have indicated that motivation is
itself curvilinearly related to achievement, with people who
have optimally high levels of motivation tending to do better
than people who are either under- or over-motivated.

Taking into account this curvilinearity, we might predict
optimal learning when difficulty level was either 25% or 75%,
rather than 50% (in other words, when motivation was
medium strong rather than maximally strong). Taking into
account the cognitive strain factor and the fact that school
learning does involve cognitive work, we would predict that
the 75% success rate material would be much more likely to
produce optimal learning than the 25% success rate material.
In fact, this is almost exactly what we found. There undoubtedly is no exact "magic percentage," since we would
expect some changes depending upon the interest in and
aptitude for the subject matter that an individual student
had, as well as general differences in ability and achievement.
However, the 75% figures seem to be a good rough estimate,
to be adjusted upward or downward depending upon these
other factors. Moving away from percentages, we would
summarize by stating that new input is at the optimal difficulty level when the student makes as rapid progress as he
can without becoming frustrated due to cognitive strain.

Crawford (1975) conducted two experimental studies
designed to follow up these correlational results through

systematic variation of the difficulty level of learning materials. He found a direct linear relationship between easiness of materials and degree of mastery, just as errorless learning advocates would predict. However, he also found a trend of increasing difficulty level associated with higher gains for high GPA subjects, as opposed to ineffectiveness of difficult materials when used by low GPA subjects.

It is difficult to draw clear implications here, since Crawford's subjects were college students working independently with printed learning materials, while our data come from early elementary school children responding orally to questions from their teachers. However, the two data sets, in combination with other considerations, seem to mutually support the idea that the learner's need for monitoring and feedback (as opposed to his ability to complete assignments successfully without help) is a major variable determining what the optimal difficulty level should be.

Regardless of age or grade level, it seems intuitively obvious that learning assignments must be easy (i.e., the student probably can complete them without help) in situations where the student will be expected to work alone with little or no opportunity to get feedback and/or help. In contrast, when the teacher or other resources are available to present material and interact with students (either in group lessons or in individual interactions concerning work assignments), it is possible and apparently optimal for the teacher to present newer, more challenging, and more difficult material. The same students might not learn it clearly working on their own, but the teacher's presence makes it possible for them to ask questions, to get feedback, and generally to have the material presented to them in ways that they can understand.

A related principle to the one concerning availability of a teacher to provide feedback concerns the ability and knowledge levels of the learners. The higher these are, the more difficult and challenging the task can become without losing effectiveness. Conversely, less able or knowledgeable students will need the material presented in smaller chunks and with greater redundancy. These generalizations seem consistent both with our own correlational data from elementary classrooms and with Crawford's (1975) experimental data from college students working independently.

Many of our findings concerning difficulty level of questions and assignments fit in with this general interpretation. Thus, for example, the more successful teachers in the low SES schools moved at a relatively slow pace and spent much time teaching and reteaching the basic fundamentals of reading, writing, and arithmetic. Most assignments were at the level of skill practice and factual memory. In contrast, the more successful high SES teachers blended in some problem solving and other high level activities which involved application of the skills as well as mastery of the skills themselves. They also worked at a faster pace and introduced more variety in their teaching methods and materials. For them, providing the students with interesting variety and stimulating challenges in their assignments was more important than seeing that they got continual and cumulative practice in mastering the fundamentals (since many already had mastered the fundamentals, at least by third grade).

Observer ratings of *assignment difficulty* showed an interesting contrast in patterns of correlation with learning gains by SES. In low SES classrooms, negative correlations were obtained between rating of assignments as being too hard and measures of student learning gains. In contrast, ratings of assignments as being too easy correlated negatively with learning gains in high SES schools. Here again is evidence that it was important for the low SES teachers to concentrate on teaching to the point of overlearning, but important for high SES teachers to move at a faster pace and provide more variety and challenge. It was especially important for teachers in low SES schools to err (if they erred at all) on the side of over-dwelling on work too long rather than on the side of moving on too quickly. It was clear that students in low SES schools simply gave up when work was too hard, withdrawing into daydreams or copying from their neighbors. This is probably yet another aspect of locus of control; these students apparently did not think that they could master the material (students who did think so would go to the teacher for help and persist in trying to figure it out rather than withdrawing from it or simply copying).

An interesting finding that has both methodological

implications for educational research and self-monitoring implications for teachers was a difference in the correlational patterns for the ratings of degree of student engagement in work assignments as opposed to those for the ratings of degree of student attention to the teacher during lessons. Ratings of student engagement in work showed strong and consistent positive correlations with learning gains, but ratings of student attention to the teacher during lessons showed little or no correlation at all. The latter finding is not unique, Taylor (1968) also found that observer ratings of students' *apparent attention* to the teacher did not correlate at all with the students' own reports of their attention or with a test of recall for the lesson administered the next day.

Apparently, even students as young as those in the second and third grades have learned how to look like they are paying attention, whether they are or not. One implication of this is that apparent student attention is not a reliable index of anything. If a teacher wants to be sure that students are following a lesson and/or understanding it, she will have to question the students or otherwise get responses from them. Students *responses* are reliable indexes, but apparent student attention is not.

In the same vein, ratings of student engagement in seat-work assignments were reliable indexes, apparently because students who appeared to be working on their assignments actually were working on them, and students who obviously were not working on their assignments clearly were not benefiting from them. Part of the reason for the difference in the relative importance and usefulness of these two aspects of student behavior as predictors of student learning probably resides in the nature of learning at these age levels. Piaget and others have shown that young children learn by doing, and it is obvious that the curriculum in the early elementary years is heavily laden with skill learning, which requires considerable repetition and practice.

Thus, both to find out if the student is progressing, and also to make sure that he does, it is necessary to see that the student gets a lot of practice in trying out new things that he is being taught. It is not sufficient to have him watch a demonstration; *he must do it himself*, and usually do it repeatedly until he can do it effortlessly. Seatwork assignments have these qualities; student attention (or apparent student attention) during lessons does not.

Also, the factor of the teacher's vigilance is probably also involved here. Teachers almost always monitor the group or class during lessons to make sure that students are paying attention and to watch for signs of confusion. Consequently, children have learned to maintain the appearance of close attention (and probably also of clear understanding!) during these times. In contrast, when they are doing seatwork, they usually are working without being closely monitored by the teacher, who usually is busy teaching a reading group. Thus, student behavior during seatwork times is an excellent indication of a complex of interrelated factors which are related to teacher effectiveness in producing student learning gains: appropriateness of assignments, interest value of assignments, willingness of students to persist in trying to do the work, and student reactions when a problem that they cannot solve on their own is encountered.

It is important that teachers became informed about these findings, because, as might have been expected on the basis of common sense, our data revealed that most teachers use apparent attention and apparent understanding as guides for making decisions about pacing lessons. While this is sufficient for many students, our findings and those of Taylor (1968) indicate that it will not work with all students. To find out unambiguously whether or not students really understand, teachers must ask questions or observe student attempts to carry out a learning task. Teachers who do this habitually will find that many students who appeared to have been attentive and to have understood a presentation are unable to apply the new material successfully by answering questions or doing exercises correctly. Thus, when we speak of "monitoring" student learning progress, we mean *getting responses*, not merely watching facial expressions for signs of inattention or confusion.

We close this chapter with a cautionary note similar to the one at the end of the previous chapter. That is, teachers should bear in mind that, to the extent that they use and succeed with teaching strategies that are appropriate for the least competent learners that they teach, those very same strategies will become decreasingly appropriate. That is, in the early stages, when a student is having difficulty with even simple assignments involving basic tool skills, it will be important to teach him in very small steps to the point of overlearning and to drill him on fundamentals. However, as he masters these fundamentals, it will be important to gradually phase in problem solving, faster pacing, more variety, and other aspects of teaching that are more *optimal for the kind of student that he has now become.*

Just as classroom rules that might have been necessary for a given classroom at a given time eventually become obsolete, teaching approaches that are based on the initially correct assumption that students must start at ground zero and take things very slowly also eventually become obsolete as the students begin to learn. Thus, matching instruction to student needs is an evolutionary, continually changing and challenging process.

Diagnosis and Evaluation

6

Information about teachers' views and behavior in the areas of diagnosis and evaluation was gathered through questionnaire and interview techniques. There were few surprises here. This was partly because teachers were in strong agreement on most points, tending to see diagnosis as important and evaluation as useful, and also to agree that evaluation should be used primarily for diagnosis and reteaching purposes rather than simply for assigning grades. Few of the teachers saw testing as particularly important, and few tested very often, at least in any formal sense.

The findings might have been somewhat different if the sample had included teachers working with some of the newer curriculum packages that feature frequent testing with associated individualized teaching modules.

However, these teachers were working within more traditional contexts and were using more traditional curricula and
methods. Some of them did have access to some of the newer
individualized packages, but they used them for enrichment
and remediation purposes rather than as their major vehicle
of instruction.

Most teachers agreed that I.Q. was important, and also
that it was important for teachers to know a child's I.Q. in
judging what was appropriate for him and how much they
could expect of him. This is reminiscent, of course, of the
"Pygmalion effect," as described by Rosenthal and Jacobson
(1968). They suggested that ideas about a child's intelligence
could cause teachers to form positive or negative expectations about his learning potential, and, through self-fulfilling
prophecy effects, ultimately affect the degree to which the
child actually learned. Subsequent research in this controversial area has shown that such effects do exist, although they
usually are not particularly strong and are more likely to
affect school achievement than measured intelligence
(Brophy and Good, 1974).

However, whether or not they had heard of this research, teachers in our study did not tend to overreact to I.Q.
scores or to suggest hard and fast one-to-one relationships between intelligence and achievement scores. They saw I.Q. as
a useful index that told something about the child and that
needed to be taken into account in planning learning experiences for him, but they ordinarily did not view it as a
fixed index that placed narrow limits upon what the child
could or should do.

Although they agreed concerning the importance of I.Q.
tests, effective teachers disagreed about the usefulness of
standardized achievement tests, depending upon whether or
not they taught in low or in high SES schools. Teachers in
high SES schools had much more faith in and were much
more positively disposed toward standardized achievement tests. This attitude probably was appropriate, considering that both the curricula and the tests connected with them
were developed with middle class children in mind, and
seemed to work reasonably well with these children. Consequently, successful high SES teachers stressed teaching the

curriculum itself and also stressed testing as an important activity along with teaching.

Low SES successful teachers agreed that evaluation and monitoring of student performance was important, but they distrusted standardized test scores. Many stated that standardized tests were essentially useless for their children, because they assumed reading abilities or test taking skills that the children simply did not have. Consequently, they substituted teacher-made tests based upon their own experiences to use in judging what abilities a child did and did not possess and how well he was progressing as the year went on. They also stressed informal evaluation conducted through observation and monitoring of seatwork. This was in addition to, and in some cases in preference to, scores obtained through formal tests, especially standardized tests.

Teachers in general felt that I.Q. was important but was not the only or even the best indicator of student potential, and that more specific information was needed in order to know what skills a child had mastered and what content was appropriate for him at a particular time. Low SES successful teachers were particularly sensitive to the dangers of overreacting to test scores that might be invalid because a child did not possess certain abilities that the test assumed. Also, successful teachers at all SES levels were sensitive to the dangers of committing logical errors such as believing that a child would succeed in one area because he had tested out well in a related area. These teachers were quite aware that children show very uneven patterns of achievement, and that a given score on a given test, even something labeled an I.Q. test, was not necessarily a reliable indicator of probable success on another test or on a particular learning task. Thus, they took the attitude that specific learning required specific evaluation, and, in the case of low SES teachers, that evaluation often would take the form of observation or checking of seatwork rather than administration of formal tests.

As a result, few teachers tested in any formal sense very often. The major exceptions to this were spelling tests. Most teachers gave a spelling test either daily or about three times a week, as a way to make sure that the children studied their spelling words and to keep track of their progress in learning them. They usually had follow-up rules requiring the children to copy out words that they missed, and, in some cases, to retake the tests or work on other activities using their week's words. In any case, spelling tests were so short and easy to administer, and so obviously face valid, that the teachers felt comfortable in using them.

In most other subject areas, however, they conducted evaluation more through *observation* than testing. They judged reading progress by having the child read in the reading group and *taking notes* on his performance. Many teachers made elaborate and systematic notes which indicated not only the frequency of errors but the particular kinds of errors each child made. They would study these notes in order to identify repeated error patterns and periodically plan specific remedial exercises for their children. Mathematical understanding was judged partly from student responses to problems posed in lessons, but mostly from observing and correcting the children's seatwork. This would give diagnostic information about particular operations that the children needed extra work or explanation in, and the teachers would follow this up through individualized contacts and occasionally with special exercises.

Regardless of the teacher's degree of sophistication about testing (familiarity with different kinds of tests, knowing the difference between a norm referenced and a criterion referenced test, etc.), most had developed a working knowledge of the skills that a child in their grade "should" show, as well as an ability to reliably observe these skills by monitoring seatwork or student responses. Consequently, although these teachers did relatively little testing in the formal sense, they did considerable evaluation. In addition, the more successful ones followed up on this evaluation by using it to prepare specific, prescriptive, remedial exercises for children who were having difficulty with particular kinds of problems. Most of this was the result of accumulated experience rather than preservice or inservice education.

Some especially interesting findings, considering the nature of the sample of teachers included in the study, appeared in relation to questionnaire items having to do with the importance of standardized tests. Somewhat to our surprise, we found an inverse or negative relationship between success in producing student learning gains and reported teaching for the tests. That is, the teachers who stated that they were the least concerned about standardized achievement tests and about seeing that their children scored highly on them were the same teachers who were most successful in producing learning gains as measured by these tests. The same successful teachers also reported less concern and worry about evaluation by supervisors or other authority figures than did the less successful teachers. Part of this difference was a difference in basic role definitions and orientation toward the teaching task in the first place. The successful teachers were too busy worrying about getting the material across to their students and teaching them with sufficient variety and thoroughness to get the job done to have much time left over for worrying about how others would see them.

A probable additional factor was their own success, however. It is likely that they knew that they were relatively successful and thus did not have to worry about how they would look if scores on standardized tests were used to evaluate them (or if anything else was used to evaluate them, for that matter). In contrast, the less successful teachers had reason to worry about how well their children did on standardized tests and about what supervisors might think of them or how they might evaluate them, because objectively they were not doing as good a job.

In any case, our interview and questionnaire data concerning evaluation (both of teachers and of students) gave no indication whatsoever that the more effective teachers in our sample were teaching for the tests, or that their high scores might have been somewhat artificial because the tests were more appropriate for them than they were for the other teachers. If anything, the opposite was the case. They professed less concern about evaluation in general and about standardized test scores in particular, and they were much more concerned about seeing that their students learned than they were about evaluations of themselves.

In the case of the low SES successful teachers, this sometimes even meant deliberately avoiding the use of

standardized tests, on the grounds that they were not appropriate or at least were not optimally appropriate for their
students. Teachers who felt this way responded by substitu-
ting tests of their own. These same teachers also often substituted curriculum materials for the standardized curriculum
if they felt that the standardized curriculum was not doing
the job or was otherwise inappropriate for their students.
Yet, these same teachers, who seemed to be going out of
their way to substitute for the standardized curriculum and
avoid using standardized tests when they didn't feel that they
were appropriate, got the highest gains on standardized materials and voiced greater concern about how their children
were doing on standardized tests.

All of this would seem to strongly confirm the attitudes
expressed by the teachers in the interviews and on the questionnaires to the effect that tests should be used merely as
vehicles for facilitating diagnosis and remediation, and that
they have little importance in their own right beyond this. At
the day-to-day level, teachers concentrated on working to get
children to master very particular and specific subskills. At a
more global level, they were trying to make sure that the
children learned the basic operations of reading, writing,
and arithmetic. For the teachers who did this job thoroughly
and well, testing was not of any great importance. It served
only to ratify what they already knew from experience-
based observations of student work.

Public Response Opportunities

7

Our low inference coding distinguished between public response opportunities, in which the student attempted to answer a question or work out a problem in a public lesson conducted before the whole class or a subgroup, as opposed to interactions in which the teacher privately gave a single student feedback about his seatwork. The data in the present chapter deal primarily with public response opportunity situations in which the teacher asked questions and called on students to respond during a lecture or discussion or had a student go to the board to work out a problem during a public lesson.

The process-product data on public response opportunities differed drastically by SES, because the public response opportunity situation itself differed drastically by SES High SES classrooms were characterized by well motivated and competitive (perhaps overly competitive) students who were eager to respond. They raised their hands with zeal and animation and tended to speak out loudly and clearly when giving an answer. In contrast, students like these were few and far between in low SES classrooms. More typically, the teacher was confronted with a class of students who wished to avoid being put "on the spot" by being called on to make a public response. When they were called on, they often kept their eyes riveted to the floor, muttered, shrugged, or spoke in a hushed whisper. They not only were not competitive in seeking opportunities to respond, like high SES children were; they often actively attempted to avoid responding.

Even where children were not afraid to respond, other problems which prevented responses or made it difficult to maintain lesson pacing were much more frequent in low SES than in high SES classrooms. For example, inattention and other, more serious, misbehavior problems were much more common. Children were unlikely to respond appropriately in public response opportunity situations if they were not paying attention or were causing a disruption. Also, other children no doubt found it difficult to concentrate on lessons, perhaps even to hear the teacher's questions, in classrooms where misbehavior problems were frequent.

These differences meant that teachers in high versus low SES schools had to deal with contrasting sets of advantages and difficulties. A teacher working in a high SES school ordinarily would have little difficulty in getting the answer she sought, but she had to work to keep order and maintain control over the flow of responses to see that everyone respected everyone else's turn and that lessons did not become overly competitive. In contrast, teachers working in a low SES school often had to work to get any kind of response at all, let alone the correct response. Often they would have to goad students into responding rather than have to hold them back and give one another a chance. The high SES teachers had to deal with *competitiveness;* low SES teachers had to deal with anxiety and *fear of failure.*

As a result, the more successful high SES teachers conducted fast paced lessons in which they moved around the group quickly and gave a large number of students multiple opportunities to respond. On those occasions when the student who was called on to give an answer was unable to give it, they usually gave the answer themselves or moved on to another student. It was important for them to give the answer themselves, since calling on other children too often led to an unhealthy competitive rivalry as well as a rush to be the first to give a correct answer when someone else failed. These teachers also had to strongly suppress call outs, insisting that each student keep quiet when another student was answering or trying to think of an answer, instead of calling out the answer themselves or making remarks like "I know, Teacher!"

In contrast, the same kinds of lessons in low SES classrooms moved at a much slower pace. The more successful teachers patiently and doggedly worked to get responses. They had to make it clear to the students that they expected and intended to wait for a response every time they asked a question, even if the response was "I don't know." Because of widespread anxiety and fear of failure, encouraging students to respond in any fashion at all often was more important in the long run than getting the correct answer to the original question. Thus, in contrast to the findings for high SES schools, in low SES schools such behavior as encouraging student initiated comments, accepting student call outs when they were relevant, and praising a good effort even if the answer was not completely correct all were correlated with success in producing student learning gains.

Patterned Turns

The contrasts in what kinds of behavior were necessary and appropriate in the two kinds of schools boiled down to a difference in what the teachers had to do in order to get the students to pay attention to the relevant content. In high SES schools, where the problem was over-competitiveness and a tendency for the students to turn their attention from the subject matter at hand and race to be the first one to get a right answer, the teacher had to fight these competitive tendencies and try to keep the children's attention centered on the content of the lesson. In low SES schools, the teacher also had to try to keep the children's attention on the content of the lesson, but in this case she had to fight anxiety and fear of failure rather than competitiveness. The successful ones did this through a combination of providing more information, providing help in the form of lecturing and hints interspersed in their questions, and continually projecting expectations for and providing encouragement and praise for giving responses to questions.

A particularly interesting, and somewhat surprising, finding that appeared in both years of our study was that teachers who called on children to read in reading group in a "patterned" rather than "random" way tended to get better gains than teachers who did not. Most writers who mention this point counsel randomness, on the theory that children will be more alert and accountable if they must be prepared to respond at any time than they will if they know that they are going to be called on to read only a certain paragraph that they can concentrate on while other children are reading their paragraphs. However, our data flatly contradicted this. Teachers who used patterned reading turns, in which students knew in advance what the order of reading was going to be, obtained better results than those who called on children randomly.

We believe that this finding can be accounted for by the students' developmental levels and anxiety levels. For one thing, these children had not yet developed the anticipation and counting skills needed to allow them to spend time "boning up" for their particular paragraph.

Also, our informal observations suggest that patterned reading turns reduce student anxiety because everyone knows when he is going to read. In addition, two other factors might be involved here. First, the children did not appear to be "boning up" on their own particular paragraph and not paying attention to anyone else. While it is likely that this would be something of a problem in older children, children at these age levels still are sufficiently respectful of the teacher's authority and sufficiently guileless to be unlikely to invent this method of circumventing the teacher's intentions. Thus, this does not appear to be much of a problem in the early grades.

Also, observations of teachers using "random" techniques suggested that their calling on students was not really random. Instead, our observers felt that most such teachers called on certain competent students a large percentage of the time and ignored certain other students a large percentage of the time. For a variety of reasons, they wanted "good" reading demonstrated and they didn't want to embarrass poor readers. The teachers *did* say they tried not to put kids "on the spot," but they didn't discuss the advantages and disadvantages of random vs. patterned turns. No teacher stated that she used patterned turns exclusively. Thus, teachers using what are called random methods of calling on students actually may have been giving extra response opportunities to some students and fewer response opportunities to others. This is one of the mechanisms through which expectation effects operate (Brophy and Good, 1974), and one indication of relatively poor teaching.

Consideration of certain SES differences also suggests that the patterned turns method should work better in both groups. In high SES reading groups, where there was a tendency for competitiveness and striving for extra reading turns, the use of the patterned method would eliminate much unnecessary bickering and decision making about who gets to read, and it would automatically insure that everyone got an equal number of turns. In low SES classrooms, where fear of the unknown and other aspects of anxiety that calling on children randomly might produce were threats to learning, the patterned method would keep anxiety at a minimum by letting each child know clearly what and when he was going to read. Again, too, the method would insure that everyone got equal opportunities to read. Thus, in both types of schools, patterned turns would insure equal turns and also would increase the likelihood that the children would pay attention to what was going on rather than worry about extraneous matters (fighting to get a turn in high SES schools; worrying about failure in low SES schools).

Clarity

The clarity of the teacher's presentation during lessons proved to be somewhat important, particularly for low SES children, although not as important as had been predicted on the basis of earlier findings with older students. Perhaps the complexity levels of the material taught at these grade levels is low enough that clarity is not a major consideration, as much as it is for teaching certain subjects at higher grade levels, particularly difficult subjects with much abstract content. In general, it seems reasonable to suppose that teacher clarity becomes increasingly important as the curriculum becomes more complex.

Practice and Feedback

Even more important than clarity (again, especially for low SES children) were opportunities for immediate practice of the skills that had just been demonstrated by the teacher, along with opportunities for immediate corrective feedback. Thus, the most successful teachers, particularly in low SES schools, conducted group lessons by giving initial demonstrations and then quickly moving around, having each student try out what had been demonstrated, and providing feedback on an individual basis. Teachers who simply gave demonstrations but did not provide the students with an opportunity to practice and get feedback, and teachers who had them practice but did not carefully monitor each individual and give individual feedback, were not nearly as successful as those who did.

The reason these variables were so much more important for low SES than for high SES children probably is the difference in pre-existing knowledge between students in the two types of schools. Many of the things taught in the lessons in high SES schools already were known by a fair portion of the students being taught that particular content on that particular day, so that these teachers often were not really teaching the children new material. Thus, even if the teachers failed to sufficiently explain the new concept and provide appropriate help to the children who didn't already know it, these children usually could get help from someone else who did already know it.

This was not the situation in low SES schools, where the material being presented often was mostly or entirely new to the entire group. Under these circumstances, it is extremely important that the children "get off to a good start" in practicing the new concept or skill. With the kinds of skills being taught to children of these ages, the main teaching problem usually is to get across the basic concepts or basic steps in performing the skill. Once the children have that much down, they can practice to the point of overlearning by working on their own. This method works well so long as the children do in fact get down the basic concepts or set of steps involved in performing the skill correctly. If they do not get these down correctly, any practice they do on their own will amount to practice of errors, and they may well end up more confused after the lesson than they were before. Thus, these children, who are so dependent upon the teacher for learning at this stage, require a clear demonstration of the concept or skill, followed closely by an opportunity to practice it themselves and to get corrective feedback from the teacher on an individual basis.

Pacing

The differences in the children's willingness and readiness to respond to questions, combined with the differences in their needs for individualized monitoring and corrective feedback, made a large difference in the optimal pacing of lessons in low vs. high SES schools. As a general rule, it was better for teachers in low SES schools to teach less, but to teach it thoroughly to the point of overlearning, than to try to move too fast and leave some children confused. It also was important to work on the children's willingness to make responses, even when they were unsure or did not know the answer. Thus, it also was important for teachers to work at a slow pace because, in addition to trying to get the answers themselves, they were working to get the children to make responses of any kind.

In contrast, lessons taught by successful high SES teachers typically moved at a brisk pace. This ordinarily worked well because the children usually knew most of the answers and because they were likely to get restless and distracted if forced to wait too long for someone to try to think out a problem and come up with a response.

Seeking Improved Responses

Furthermore, attempting to improve responses (get some kind of answer from a child who made no response or said "I don't know" the first time, or getting a more complete or higher level answer from a student who gave an incomplete or lower level answer the first time), although mildly positively correlated with learning gains in low SES schools, was negatively correlated with learning gains in high SES schools. This seemed surprising at first, since getting students to improve their responses is a teacher skill that many teacher educators stress as important, but upon reflection our findings make sense.

Given that most of the high SES children already knew most of the answers to most of the questions that were asked, and given that they usually were eager (if not overly eager) to respond, attempting to get them to improve on initial responses usually amounted to pointless pumping. These children were unlikely to be able to improve their responses in most situations, because if they knew the answer they would have given it in the first place (gleefully!).

In contrast, it was useful to try to get students to improve their responses relatively more often in low SES schools. Where students in these schools did not respond correctly the first time, it often was because they were afraid to take a chance, rather than because they didn't know the answer. Thus, in situations where the teacher judges that the child might and probably does know the answer, it is a good idea to try to get an improved response. However, in cases where it is clear that the child gave what he thought was the answer and is wrong, attempts to get him to improve it are unlikely to succeed, unless the teacher provides substantial help in the form of clues or hints.

When teachers did try to improve responses, it definitely was more helpful to the students if they provided clues or hints or a simpler question than if they simply repeated the question without providing any additional help. Again, the latter boils down to pointless pumping. Simply repeating the question accomplishes nothing except in cases where the student has not heard it the first time. If the student clearly has heard the question but has not answered it, it is because he does not know the answer rather than because he is unwilling to give the answer, in most cases. This was even true in low SES clssrooms, with the exception of the most anxious and fearful students. Even with the latter, however, simply repeating questions usually only made them more anxious, so that the teacher had to provide some form of encouragement or help if she wanted to get a response. Often, simplifying by asking an easier question was more successful than attempting to help by giving hints or clues.

One exception to this occurred with regard to reading instruction, where *phonics clues* (telling the child the sound of the word, asking what the first sound was, providing the first sound for him to get him started, etc.) were particularly useful for children in general and low SES children in particular. If the child were reasonably likely to benefit from the clue, it usually was preferable to give him a phonics clue in situations where he was stuck on a word in reading group than to simply tell him the word or to call on someone else to provide it. This served the multiple purposes of making the response easier for the student, giving him a place to start, and reinforcing the expectation that the student would make a response every time he was called on.

Waiting for Responses

The time spans involved here, particularly for the time

elapsing between a question, a response, and reactive feedback from the teacher, were very small. Rowe (1972) found that only three of the 35 elementary school teachers that she timed would wait as long as three seconds for a response from a student before doing something themselves, and that they had great difficulty in learning to prolong their waiting time. After getting them to prolong their waiting times, however, she found improved classroom atmospheres and improved learning. However, these were high SES classrooms. Our data, in combination with hers and with the considerations outlined above, suggest that it is important to give the student a chance to think out a response, and perhaps also to provide some help to enable him to improve his response, *to the extent that he is likely to benefit from* this time and/or help.

This is true especially in situations where the classroom is already over-competitive and needs some socialization to the effect that an individual's response opportunity is to be respected and that he should be given time to think if he does not have the answer on the tip of his tongue when he is called on. However, in situations where the child is extremely unlikely to be able to improve his response, attempting to make him do so may be futile.

Obviously, this involves considerable judgment on the part of the teacher. Most teachers report that they make such judgments on the basis of the child's facial expression, but our data and experience suggest that this is not a very reliable criterion. A combination of the child's present appearance, along with information about his general knowledge in the area and his specific knowledge about the content at hand, would be much more reliable. However, this obviously is much more specific and presumes considerable knowledge that would be difficult to keep track of, let alone collect. In any case, a fruitful area for research and development in education is the training of teachers to know when to give an answer and move on vs. when to try to get the student to improve his original response.

SUMMARY

The public response opportunity data for low vs. high SES

schools seem disparate, and in many ways they are. However, certain main themes hold up in both sets of data. First, it is important for the teacher to keep the students focused on the content of the lesson, and not to let them get distracted with personal or interpersonal concerns having nothing to do with what is being taught. Second, it is important for the teacher to insure that the child has the basic concept or skill down when something new is being taught, so that when he practices it on his own he will be practicing appropriately. If this is not done, the student will be practicing errors and will have to do some unlearning in addition to learning the original material. Third, although high SES children need faster pacing and somewhat more challenge than low SES children, as a general rule it seems better to err on the side of over-teaching than under-teaching. This is especially so with low SES children. Fourth, it is important for the teacher to be able to judge accurately when to provide feedback and give the child the answer vs. when to try to work with him to get him to improve his response on his own. Fifth, and perhaps most important, the teacher must retain control over the flow of interaction and response opportunities in public response opportunity situations. If the teacher should abandon this control, so that the students are in effect deciding who gets to respond according to who raises their hand most often or most vociferously, an unhealthy competitiveness and a reduced learning rate will result.

Motivation and Incentives

8

As was the case with getting responses and giving feedback to students in public response opportunity situations, the data concerning motivation and incentives in the classroom showed consistent differences according to school SES. In general, the most successful low SES teachers motivated primarily through gentle and positive encouragement and praise, while the successful high SES teachers motivated through challenge and through a critical demandingness which involved communicating high expectations to their students and criticizing them for failing to meet them.

Praise

Thus, praise rarely correlated positively with

student learning in high SES schools, although it correlated positively fairly often in low SES schools. In general, though, praise did not correlate nearly as positively with learning gains as was expected on the basis of previous literature. Praise tends to be favored by teacher education textbook writers of every description, ranging from self theorists who see it as important for building self esteem, to behavior modifiers who see it as the major method of social reinforcement. However, in both years of our study, praise tended to correlate *negatively* with learning gains in high SES students and positively but very weakly with learning gains in low SES students (the nature of these correlations varied with context, however, as will be explained below).

The strongest negative correlations regarding praise were for praise which occurred in student initiated private interactions. Most of these were situations in which the student finished his assignment and then came up to the teacher to show it to her. Probably a good portion of these interactions were initiated by students who were somewhat dependent upon the teacher and perhaps overly concerned with getting praise from her. In any case, our data suggest that teachers who responded positively and did give praise in such situations were *less* successful in producing student learning gains than teachers who did not provide praise at these times. In contrast, praise during *teacher initiated* work interactions tended to correlate *positively* with student learning gains, particularly among low SES children. Our interpretation of this contextual difference involves two separate considerations.

First, the contextual difference (teacher vs. student initiation of interaction) probably made a difference in who was praised and what was praised. Teachers with especially high scores for praise in student initiated contacts probably were being "conditioned" by their more dependent and praise-seeking students to provide praise upon "demand." While this might have had some benefit to the student who sought the praise, it seems reasonable to suppose that frequent interactions of this kind could have produced classrooms marked by unhealthy competitiveness, jealousies, and over-concern with teacher praise at the expense of curriculum content.

Although data unfortunately were not available on individual students (they will be available in a later study), our observers' impressions were that a large majority of the student initiated interactions which led to teacher praise were initiated by a small number of students who dominated the teacher's attention. Where a greater proportion of teacher praise was given during teacher initiated interactions, the praise seemed to be spread around more evenly among the students.

A second factor connected with the contextual difference of teacher vs. student initiation of the interaction concerns the quality of the praise. Again, although systematic data were not available (but will be after a present study is completed), our observers believed that teacher praise in student initiated situations tended to be brief, perfunctory, and generally lacking in both affect and specificity. In contrast, praise occurring in teacher initiated interactions tended to be more specific (the teacher indicated in some detail what it was about the student's work that was praiseworthy, as opposed to giving the student a perfunctory "That's good"), and it tended to be delivered in a manner that suggested more credibility and positive affect.

A third factor that could have made a difference in these findings concerning praise can be extrapolated from child development literature (Weiner and Kukla, 1970). These investigators discovered an interaction between achievement motivation and the effects of praise vs. criticism on children. Those with high achievement motivation and a generally successful record of achievement (corresponding roughly to the high SES students in our study) responded better to criticism than to praise, while those with lower achievement motivation and lower actual achievement (corresponding roughly to the low SES students in our study) responded much better to praise than to criticism.

In short, a student who is accustomed to success, expects success, and is capable of achieving success with reasonable effort tends to respond well, at least in terms of improved achievement, to chiding criticism for failure that results from lack of effort or persistent application of skills. In contrast, the student who is accustomed to failure, expects failure, and has difficulty mastering something even if he persists long and hard is much more likely to be positively affected by encouragement and praise, and more likely to be negatively affected by criticism.

Thus, there are several mutually supportive explanations for the lack of strong positive correlations for praise, and even for the negative correlations occurring in the high SES schools, despite the overwhelming tendency to stress praise as an important teacher technique in the literature. We accept what our data say, although we would caution against over-reacting to them, and particularly against telling teachers not to praise their students. Instead, we think it is important to stress that praise should be individualized and genuine, and that whatever it is that the teacher wishes to praise should be specified in the process of giving the praise, so that the praise does in fact function as a positive incentive or motivator for the student.

Also, it appears important that praise should be given privately, in order to minimize tendencies to create an un-healthy classroom atmosphere by engendering jealousies or holding up certain students as "pets" or examples for their classmates. We suspect that students receiving this kind of praise do not experience it as rewarding, since it might subject them to jealousy and perhaps even anger or physical attack from classmates. Also, the classmates who observe such praise seem less likely to be positively motivated by it (as would be suggested by the vicarious reinforcement principle) and more likely to be irritated by it.

One implication here is that application of the behavior modification principle of motivating one student by praising the desirable behavior of another is trickier than it may seem at first, because factors other than noticing and praising good behavior need to be taken into account. First, it seems important that the praise be initiated by the teacher, not the student. Second, it seems to be important that the teacher praise in a way that focuses attention on the desirable be-havior and minimizes the probability that anyone will per-ceive the interaction as the teacher showing favoritism toward a "pet" student.

Third, it seems reasonable to suggest that praise should

be couched in terms of the student's present progress relative to his past progress, and not in terms of the student's achievement relative to his classmates. The former type of praise focuses attention on what the student has done rather than upon the student himself, personally, and it is equally applicable to all of the students in the classroom (i.e., regardless of whatever individual differences in levels of progress there may be, any student who makes any kind of progress can be praised for the progress he has made, given his level). In contrast, the second kind of praise implicitly sets up a competitive situation in which students who hear it get the message that the only way they can get praise is to outperform or at least do as well as the student who has just been praised. For many students, this will not be probable or even possible. As a result, such praise could have a depressing and discouraging effect rather than a positively motivating one.

Our stress on the importance of making praise *credible* and *genuine* also draws some support from the child development literature. Several researchers have found that young school age children are differentially sensitive to praise and criticism depending upon what kind of adult it comes from. Criticism tends to have mixed effects whether it comes from male or female adults, but praise tends to be more motivating when it comes from male adults. To put it another way, many young children apparently "tune out" the verbal praise of female adults. Perhaps they are so accustomed to it that it no longer functions as motivation, or perhaps they have good reason not to trust it or to put any great importance upon it (this interpretation is supported by data showing that praise from high status adults is more effective than praise from low status adults, and males usually have more status in the eyes of children than females). In any case, data from several sources agree in suggesting that verbal praise from female teachers simply is not very motivating for young school children.

The exceptions in our data fit in neatly with the available literature. Praise showed positive correlations in teacher initiated private interactions and in reactions to student answers to opinion questions. The former finding suggests the importance of the genuineness factor, while the latter finding suggests the importance of encouraging students who are hesitant or fearful.

Perhaps if we had been able to collect data on individual students and/or to collect data on the qualitative aspects of praise rather than simply the frequency of it, the praise data might have come out more positively. In any case, it is clear that the teachers as a group were not praising very effectively. This was especially true for the teachers in high SES schools, where praise never correlated with student learning gains and where there were relatively high ratings of student passivity and withdrawal (that is, although many and perhaps most of the students were enthusiastically and perhaps overly competitive, a subset of students had become discouraged and alienated from the teaching-learning process and were rather apathetic and passive in the classroom). The teachers clearly were unsuccessful in motivating these students adequately.

Symbolic Rewards

The use of symbolic rewards, particularly gold stars and smiling faces placed upon papers to be taken home and shown to the parents, or placed on charts in the room, showed consistent positive associations with learning gains. Apparently, the children were still young enough so that symbolic rewards of this kind were positively motivating. All kinds of involvement of the parents in partnership with the teachers and the school were considered to be important and useful by the teachers, particularly in low SES schools where involvement was more difficult for the parents and the communication gap between school and home was wider. Arranging for positive experiences such as these, in which children could bring home good work and get praise and encouragement from the parents, was considered to be (and apparently was) especially valuable.

No data were available on the use of concrete rewards or their symbolic substitutes, tokens. This was because tokens and concrete rewards were not used in any systematic way by the teachers under study. Both the teachers and the curricula they used were relatively traditional, and no one was systematically implementing a token economy or even a reasonable facsimile of a token economy. A few teachers were using opportunities to work in various learning centers as "rewards" for successfully finishing assignments, but there were not enough data on this practice to allow any conclusions concerning its relationships to student learning gains.

Verbal praise from the teachers was not the only type of "reward" that was ineffective. The technique of "rewarding" students by "allowing" them to perform housekeeping chores or assume monitor duties was consistently negatively associated with student learning gains. Apparently, even these young students, despite their general adult orientation and desire to please, did not experience such "rewards" as positively motivating. In fact, the data suggest that teachers who relied on this method heavily actually might have been punishing good work (or at least efficient work) by their students, in effect training them to work more slowly or at least to avoid letting them know when they were finished.

The positive results for such behaviors as letting the children go to a learning center or engage in some other self chosen activity upon completion of assignments indicate that the general idea of using privileges as rewards can be successful, but thse specific findings concerning housekeeping and monitor jobs indicate that the children did not consider these as "privileges."

In summary, symbolic rewards, particularly when tied to the operation of taking good work home for parents to inspect, proved to be positively associated with learning gains in both low and high SES schools. This was in sharp contrast to verbal praise from the teacher, which was not associated with learning gains in high SES schools and only weakly positively associated with learning gains in low SES schools. It seems likely that this finding is at least partially a function of the ages of the children; we do not believe that symbolic rewards such as stars or smiling faces would be positively motivating to older students, although symbolic rewards more suitable to the students' ages or levels of development might be.

Criticism

One of the most widely reported and consistently replicated findings in process-product educational research is that criticism correlates negatively with student achievement. However, as noted above, data from child development research suggests an interactional relationship rather than a negative one, and our own findings did indeed reveal interactional relationships and also contextual effects. We believe that we can explain the apparent discrepancies, but first let us describe the nature of the criticism findings in some detail, so that readers are clear about what they both do and do not imply.

First, it should be kept in mind that criticism was relatively infrequent, both in its own right and in relationship to praise. Furthermore, even the most critical teachers operated within a general context of warmth and student orientation, for the most part. Thus, positive correlations between criticism and student learning gains do not mean that the most successful teachers were hypercritical; they mean that the more successful teachers in high SES schools occasionally would criticize a child for poor performance in contrast to the less successful teachers who rarely or never criticized a child regardless of how poor or inappropriate his performance was. Finally, it should be noted that the criticism measures which correlated positively with student learning gains were confined to criticism of poor responses to questions, poor performance in reading turns, and poor seatwork. That is, they were *criticisms for poor academic work.*

This pattern of positive relationships between criticism and student learning gains did *not* hold up for behavioral criticism or for any other forms of negative teacher behavior related to anything other than inadequate student performance on academic tasks. Thus, the kind of criticism that we are talking about when we say that criticism correlated positively with student learning gains was criticism for poor academic work. Furthermore, casual observations by our observers suggest that such criticism usually was appropriate, as when teachers criticized children for doing sloppy work or for not paying attention. The latter type of criticism usually only occurred after one or more warnings had preceded it, so that the student in effect was "asking for it."

The outcome of all this is a naturalistic replication in an educational setting of Weiner and Kukla's (1970) findings concerning the interaction of praise and criticism with student achievement levels and achievement motivation in determining the effects of these adult verbal behaviors on student motivation. It appears that criticism which involves gently but firmly chiding a child for working clearly below his capacity and/or for working sloppily has a positively motivating effect on high achieving children with high achievement motivation (assuming that we can extrapolate this meaning from the SES differences in our data). However, it should be kept in mind that this positive relationship between criticism and student learning gains was obtained only with students who fit this description, only with criticism of academic work, and only when the criticism appeared to be justified and was used relatively infrequently.

The general bulk of our data, as well as the overwhelming evidence from both laboratory and naturalistic field studies in psychology and education, suggest that an approach to motivation which features positive expectations and positive reinforcement, with minimal attention to negative behaviors, is optimal. However, contrary to the dictates of those who would over-simplify behavior modification principles, our data suggest that not all undesirable student behavior should be ignored. Student behavior which is under the control of the student (i.e., he could easily change it if he wanted to), which is clearly inappropriate (i.e., the student "knows better"), and which has persisted despite a combination of positive and encouraging intervention efforts with ignoring inappropriate behavior, calls for some negative intervention in the form of criticism.

Such criticism appears to be increasingly desirable to the extent that the student has a strong self concept and clearly is underachieving due to lack of sufficient concentration or effort. We recommend its use in these instances, although we would caution teachers that it is better to err on the side of giving the student the benefit of the doubt than to err on the side of jumping to conclusions and perhaps upsetting or

alienating the student unnecessarily, and we also would repeat once again that such criticism is likely to be effective
only if it occurs within a broad general context of warmth
and student orientation on the part of the teacher.

Thus, under the conditions mentioned above, it may
sometimes be appropriate for a teacher to chide a student
with a comment like:

"George, slow down and work more carefully—you're
making mistakes because you're trying to go too fast."

"Mary, don't try to guess the answer ahead of time—lis-
ten to the question and think about it before you try to
answer it."

"Jimmy, stop copying from Sam and do your own
work; I'm warning you for the last time!"

Such criticism seems appropriate, because it suits the
situation and tells the child what he should be doing in addition to criticizing his inappropriate behavior. In contrast,
hypercritical reactions like "That's a dumb answer—What's
the matter with you?" would be inappropriate. Such powerful and rejecting criticism seems more likely to produce
resentment than motivation to improve.

Punishment

The findings concerning punishment are similar, for the
most part, to the findings concerning criticism. First, as
noted in Chapter 4, the most successful classroom managers
were those who organized their classrooms effectively and
provided their students with appropriate assignments and
materials, so that they kept the students actively engaged in
meaningful work for the vast majority of the time, thus
minimizing the rates of misbehavior and the need for punishment. However, when punishment was necessary, certain
forms of punishment were more useful than others, and the
effectiveness of punishment differed according to the SES
of the school.

Among the general findings across SES levels, the most
important was the one mentioned already: avoiding the need

to punish was much more effective than knowing how to punish effectively. A second general finding already mentioned was that relatively mild punishments which involved giving the student information about what was wrong with his behavior and how he should change were more effective than more extreme punishments, particularly punishments which did not involve instructions about how behavior should be changed. Simple warnings and other reactions geared toward changing student behavior were more effective than severe threats or punishment.

For high SES students only, scolding showed occasional positive correlations with student learning gains. This appeared to be part of the general pattern already discussed in some detail: all students flourished best under relatively warm and student oriented teachers, but high SES students (and probably particularly students with high self esteem and high abilities who tended to goof off occasionally) seemed to improve when criticized or scolded for inappropriate behavior, especially for inappropriate work on assignments.

However, the most effective forms of punishment were not really punishments at all. Instead, they were actions such as keeping the child after school or arranging for an individual conference with him in order to discuss his misbehavior and come to some kind of agreement about how the problem was to be resolved.

Usually, these conferences did not involve any actual punishment, although they sometimes did involve threats of punishment if the student did not respond by changing his behavior to make it more appropriate. Strong punishments, such as spanking or other physical punishment, and strong personal criticism were either unrelated or negatively related to student learning gains. The same was true for teacher attempts to "pass the buck" to someone else by sending the child to the principal or to a school counselor for "discipline." In short, in high SES schools the more successful teachers recognized that problems occurring in the classroom had to be handled by them, and they tended to handle them in individualized ways that were geared to get the problem out for discussion and resolution, as opposed to either trying to avoid the problem by shunting it off to someone else or to overreacting with strong negative punishments.

In low SES schools, contrary to what many might have predicted, punishment appeared to be relatively unimportant. No form of punishment correlated positively or negatively with student learning gains. We suspect that this would not be the case at higher grade levels, where simply establishing authority in the classroom can be a major task for the teacher. However, in these early grades, the children in low SES schools were primarily passive, anxious, and alienated from learning, so that the teachers had to contend with problems of low self concept and a tendency to withdraw from anxiety-producing situations, rather than with disruptions or challenges to their authority. Consequently, teachers working in low SES schools in these early grades were most successful if they concentrated their efforts on establishing close, warm relationships with their students, providing their students with the encouragement that they needed in order to work consistently at mastering the curriculum, and matching their students' needs and interests with appropriate assignments and materials.

Punishment is primarily a vehicle for stopping the occurrence of objectionable behavior; it is not useful for getting the individual to start some new behavior. We suspect that this is why it was relatively unimportant at these grade levels in the low SES schools in contrast to the high SES schools. In high SES schools, the children were active, and sometimes children who consistently acted out in undesirable ways had to be disciplined through criticism, scolding, or punishment. In low SES schools, in contrast, such acting out was rare at these grade levels, and the teacher had to instead concentrate on getting the students to do things in a positive way rather than to get them to stop doing negative or undesirable things.

Finally, a general finding worth mentioning was that assigning normal school work as punishment was negatively correlated with student learning gains. This seems obvious, although it is done more frequently than might be imagined. In brief, this is an extremely self-defeating practice because it creates or reinforces in the student the idea that ordinary school work is to be detested and avoided if at all possible.

After all, if it is something that the teacher assigns as punishment, why would anybody want to do it voluntarily? Thus, while under some circumstances there *might* be some point in a punishment such as having a student write out "I must pay attention during reading group" ten or fifteen times, we see no justification under any circumstances for the assignment of ordinary school work as punishment.

SUMMARY

Beyond the general findings reported in Chapter 4 to the effect that the more successful teachers organize their classrooms so as to avoid having to punish very often and that behavioral interventions which involve calling attention to misbehavior and giving instructions about how behavior should be changed were more effective than non-instructive punishments, the data on motivation, incentives, and punishment differed considerably by school SES.

In high SES classrooms, where the students were generally high achieving and well motivated, sometimes to the point of being overly competitive, the teachers' main task was to provide a variety of challenging stimulation in assignments for the children. Praise, particularly praise of students who approached the teacher seeking it, proved to be negatively related to student learning gains. In contrast, criticism of students for poor work was positively related to learning gains. Symbolic rewards such as stars and smiling faces were effective motivators, but teacher verbal praise and attempts to "reward" children by allowing them to perform monitor duties were not. Although scolding sometimes was effective, the most effective ways of dealing with misbehavior were to have individual conferences with the child or keep him after school to discuss the problem and state expectations for behavioral change, as opposed to more punitive and less informative methods which were negatively related to learning gains.

In contrast, the students in low SES schools were primarily apathetic, anxious, and alienated from learning.

Neither rewards nor punishments were particularly important one way or the other in these schools. What was important was the teacher's ability to motivate the students to become actively engaged in the learning process to the point that they would answer questions in public response situations and work persistently on their seatwork. The most successful teachers did this through a combination of providing a warm, supportive atmosphere, praising students (but doing so mostly in teacher initiated individual contacts), and matching demands and materials to the needs and interests of the students.

Successful teachers in both kinds of schools communicated high expectations, but the successful teachers in high SES schools did so through a critical demandingness, while the successful teachers in low SES schools did so through patience and encouragement.

It was our impression that praise, to the extent that it was effective at all, was effective when given in teacher initiated, private interactions with the student and when it called attention to the student's specific advances over previous levels of knowledge or skill, as opposed to calling attention to the student's standing relative to his classmates. Praise given in response to a student initiated request for it, particularly when it led to a public "fuss" in the classroom, was maladaptive. Reward methods which allowed the student to take home examples of good work to show the parent seemed to be especially effective, both because the students seemed to experience them as particularly rewarding and because they helped engender positive expectations and attitudes in the parents concerning their child and his schoolwork.

Taken together, the data on praise and criticism suggest some interesting relationships between these teacher motivational variables and teachers' expectations for students. All in all, it appears that a tendency to criticize a student for a poor answer or for poor work is associated with high expectations for that student, and, conversely, that unusually high rates of teacher praise might be expressions of low expectations for a student (attempts to compensate for poor performance by making it up to the student through praising what he does well, attempts to encourage the student, etc.). Of course, we must note again that these observations apply only within the broader context of a warm and supportive teacher-student relationship; they do not imply that teachers should minimize praise and maximize criticism. Nevertheless, rates of praise and criticism sometimes are used as "face valid" measures of appropriate teacher behavior, because it seems obvious that praising children is good and criticizing them is bad. However, our data suggest that the situation is not this simple, and that, under certain circumstances, *relatively* low rates of praise and high rates of criticism can indicate both good student performance and good teacher-student relationships.

Some Surprises

9

The major findings concerning relationships between teacher characteristics and student learning gains now have been presented. However, before moving on to discuss their implications, we want to mention a series of variables which did *not* relate to student learning gains. These negative findings are of some importance and are described here because previous research on process-product relationships has consistently supported their importance as correlates of teacher effectiveness. Others are included because they have been advocated strongly by educational theorists, although they do not necessarily have much empirical backing.

Teacher Affect

One of the most pervasive and basic aspects of

the teacher's personality, which we expected to correlate with student learning gains, was her affectionateness toward the children. We thought that the warmer, more affectionate teachers generally would be more effective than other teachers, particularly in low SES schools. As it turned out, teacher affectionateness did not show this relationship. It was unrelated, either linearly or curvilinearly, to students' learning gains.

The same was true for teacher enthusiasm, a variable that most previous studies have found to be positively associated with learning gains (Rosenshine and Furst, 1973; Dunkin and Biddle, 1974). We suspect that these negative findings (i.e., lack of relationships) are related to the ages of the students, and perhaps also to the variance in the teacher sample. Most of the studies supporting the variables discussed in this chapter, and in fact most of the studies on process-product relationships generally, have been conducted at higher grade levels. We believe that this is the primary reason for most of the conflicts between our findings and several findings common in the literature.

Concerning teacher affect and enthusiasm, for example, we believe that an argument can be made that they are less important with younger children than with older children, despite the acknowledged importance of adults relative to the peer group for younger children. For one thing, young children tend to accept without much questioning or opposition the idea that they are supposed to go to school and "learn," and that the teacher's job is to teach them. Respect and a certain type of affection is afforded to the teacher more or less automatically; teachers working with young children usually do not have to prove themselves the way that teachers working with older students do. Similarly, younger children tend to accept the school curriculum as given, so that enthusiasm and some of the other teacher characteristics that are important in generating interest in a subject area among older students are superfluous with younger ones. Thus, it can be argued that affect, enthusiasm, and related teacher characteristics are less important with young children, particularly those in high SES schools, than they are witn older children and adolescents. Of variables related to those teacher qualities, only ratings of teachers' showmanship showed significant (positive) correlations with learning gains, and only for low SES children.

Also, it is clear that the sample did not contain teachers who were extremely negative on these variables. That is, contrary to the unfortunate recent tendency to picture teachers as incompetent bullies who take out their frustrations on their students, our data revealed that almost all of the teachers in our sample were warm and student oriented (in varying degrees). Taking into account these various factors, perhaps it is not so surprising that teacher affect and enthusiasm were unrelated to student learning gains.

Observer comments suggested another possible reason. It was their opinion that the teachers rated extremely highly on scales of affect and enthusiasm were expressing their affect in ways that minimized their credibility and effectiveness. Some of the teachers rated highly on affect and enthusiasm were more properly described as gushy and overly theatrical than as extremely warm and enthusiastic. This was not true of all teachers rated highly on these scales, but it appeared to be true of enough of them to neutralize any tendencies that these variables might have had to correlate with student learning gains.

Finally, it should be noted again that our data did not include separate coding of teacher interactions with individual students. This was particularly important for variables like affect and enthusiasm, because these usually are expressed in interactions with individuals rather than with the class as a whole. If data had been available on the teachers' affective stance toward each student separately, rather than in terms of general class means, systematic relationships might have been revealed.

Student Characteristics

Related to the preceeding were several negative findings concerning student characteristics. First, as mentioned in Chapter 5, ratings of students' apparent attentiveness toward the teacher were mostly *unrelated* to student learning gains. Presumably, this was because apparent attention and actual attention are not that highly correlated, so that the fact that students appeared to be paying attention and following a lesson was no guarantee that they actually were doing so. Attention ratings correlated in the expected direction with learning gains only for the most extreme and chaotic classrooms, where students were not merely inattentive but were disobedient and disruptive.

Other student behavior that surprisingly did not relate to learning gains included behavior when the teacher's back was turned (business as usual vs. making faces, fooling around, baiting the teacher, etc.) and rating of classroom atmosphere (the appearance of a happy, familial feeling among the students vs. dreariness or strife). Again, the probable reasons for the absence of relationships here include both the ages of the children and the ranges of behavior observed. These children apparently have not reached the ages yet where problems of disrespect for the teacher or for one another were serious enough to affect learning gain scores. The low SES children were fearful and anxious, and the high SES children were sometimes overly competitive, but defiance of the teacher or major problems of interpersonal conflict were rare. Thus, these student variables, which are so important at higher grade levels, were essentially irrelevant at these early grades. Problems in these areas did not occur frequently enough to play much of a role in determining student learning gains or in posing major problems for the teachers.

Indirect Teaching

Negative or primarily negative findings also were obtained for several aspects of teaching which have been strongly advocated in the literature. One of these was the concept of "indirect teaching" as propounded by Flanders (1970). Flanders and his associates have conducted numerous studies supporting the contention that indirect teaching is positively (or, in some cases, curvilinearly) related to student learning gains. They also have produced much evidence that indirect teaching is strongly related to positive student attitudes. Indirect teaching usually is defined to include minimal teacher talk and maximal student talk, minimal lecture and maximal discussion, stress on independent student learning, frequent praise of students, frequent use of student ideas and inclusion of student ideas in discussions, and frequent student-to-student interaction.

For the most part, these indications of indirect teaching were either unrelated or negatively related to student learning gains, although in a few places they were beginning to show positive relationships in the high SES schools. We conclude from this that indirect teaching is inappropriate in the early elementary grades when children are still in the process of mastering the fundamental tool skills of reading, writing, and arithmetic, although it may be appropriate and even optimal for students at higher levels who are spending much time discussing material that they have read and conducting independent learning projects. In any case, the data were loud and clear in stating that indirect teaching methods are *not* associated with success in producing student learning gains in the early elementary grades.

Lesson Structure

The same was true for the use of advance organizers, the importance of clarity and proper sequencing, the importance of directing attention through appropriate questions embedded in the lesson, and other aspects of verbal learning propounded as important by Ausubel (1963). As was the case with Flanders' indirect teaching, the reason that these teaching behaviors stressed by Ausubel, which generally have been well supported in other studies, did not correlate with learning gains in the present study, was the ages of the children. In the early elementary grades, the children are mastering fundamental tool skills, and this means that most of their time is spent practicing skills to the point of overlearning, usually skills that have a heavy motor component such as writing. This is in sharp contrast to the more purely conceptual learning that goes on at higher grade levels and is taught through primarily verbal means. Thus, Ausubel's variables, which are important for verbal exposition of meaningful conceptual material, are relatively unimportant for teachers working in the early elementary grades, for the simple reason that the teaching-learning conditions in these grades do not involve much verbal exposition of purely conceptual material.

Teacher Directiveness

Other variables which have been strongly advocated in the literature by some writiers but which turned out to be utterly unrelated to student learning gains in the present study included the ratio of divergent to convergent questions and the variable of authoritarian vs. democratic classroom leadership style. The divergent/convergent questioning variable apparently was unimportant because of lack of variance in the kinds of questions asked at these grade levels, as well as the relative unimportance of questions in general at these grade levels compared to their importance in the higher grades. A smaller proportion of the teaching-learning situation in the early grades involves teacher questions and student responses, so that teacher questioning behavior is relatively less important here than it is later.

Also, the vast majority of the questions that are asked are simple factual questions that teachers in the early grades ask in the process of teaching fundamental tool skills. Very few higher order questions are asked because very little higher order material is taught (appropriately so, if we are to believe Piaget and others who suggest that the young child is not yet cognitively ready for highly abstract, purely verbal material). In short, the teacher's ability to question the children at varying cognitive levels simply is not relevant yet.

The authoritarian vs. democratic leadership style difference also is a matter of relevance. This variable has been studied many times by many different investigators. Although the data are far from clean and clear, they suggest that an authoritarian style maximizes cognitive gains while a democratic style maximizes student attitudes. In the present study, democratic leadership styles were simply unrelated to learning gains, rather than negatively related (as the major thrust of the literature would predict) or positively related (as enthusiastic advocates who refuse to look at the data would predict).

Again, the basic reason seems to be that this teacher characteristic is essentially irrelevant to children this young. The children accept the teacher's and their own roles in school without protest or even much thought, so that an authoritarian teacher is not likely to be particularly resented or even thought unusual by the children. At the same time, although the social perceptiveness and capacities for self-regulation of young children should not be underestimated, curriculum considerations and the relative immaturity of the children in these early grades make a truly democratic leadership style unfeasible, even if the teacher should desire to use it.

Perhaps none of this should be surprising. Previous research (Good and Grouws, 1975) has shown that children in the early grades tend to be mildly positive to enthusiastic about school, and to adapt to whatever quirks and personal characteristics their teacher might have. Consequently, except for teachers who are totally disorganized and inept and/or negativistic and hostile toward the children, teacher personality characteristics such as affectionateness, enthusiasm, credibility, student orientation, and leadership style are not particularly important in the early grades. They become increasingly important, however, as the children get older and more sophisticated.

Teacher Confidence

Another variable that did not show the expected (positive) correlations with learning gains was confidence. Again,

although this probably is vital for a teacher working with
older students, particularly with students who have critical,
judgmental attitudes toward the teacher, it is largely irrelevant for teachers working with young children who tend to
accept them as they are. Also, as noted above, serious
defiance of teachers was extremely rare, so that the teachers
were unlikely to undergo experiences which could shake
or test their confidence, and unlikely to have to prove themselves in situations where confidence was essential. Confidence is not particularly important in teaching young children, because they do not challenge you or force you to
prove yourself. Thus, a teacher who might be unable to
handle a rowdy class of older students might do quite well
with a class of younger ones, assuming that she had the
classroom management and instructional skills necessary to
do a good job of teaching them.

Politeness

Another variable that did not show the expected positive
relationships with student learning was teacher politeness.
High inference ratings of politeness, as well as coding of
whether or not the teacher thanked the student for running
errands or doing favors, showed either no relationships or
curvilinear relationships to learning. In part, this probably
is a special case of the more general finding that teacher
verbalizations are not very important to young children.
Also, coder observations suggested that the curvilinearity
in some of the findings might have been related to gushiness
and/or "playing favorites" by certain teachers. These teachers not only were polite, but went out of their way to make a
big fuss when asking a child to do something for them or
when thanking them for doing it. Although well intentioned,
such behavior was more likely to embarrass the child and
irritate his classmates than to have positive effects.

Seeking Improved Responses

The final set of surprising data involved aspects of obtaining and reacting to student responses to teacher questions. One issue, the matter of patterned turns vs. random turns in reading groups, already has been discussed in some detail in Chapter 7. Another aspect, the question of whether or not to stick with a student who has failed to answer a question and attempt to get him to improve his response, also has been discussed in Chapter 7, but is worth repeating and discussing further here. Once again, the data suggest a fundamental difference on these variables depending upon the ages of the children involved.

Based on research at higher grade levels, most educational writers have suggested calling upon students randomly, in order to keep them continually accountable, and staying with students to try to help them improve their responses, in order to give them time to deal with the material, build their confidence, and avoid creating undesirable competitiveness in classroom atmospheres. Again, our data suggest that these ideas, while apparently appropriate for older students, are inappropriate in the early grades. However, this time the reasons differ according to the SES levels of the schools (or, to be more accurate, according to the levels of cognitive development and competence mastery of the children).

In low SES schools, or in any school where a student is hesitant and fearful, the anxiety produced by calling on students randomly appears to wash out whatever benefits it may bring in accountability or the development of self confidence. Patterned turns help hold down anxiety in children who fear public response situations, and they also automatically insure that everyone gets an equal chance. Working for improved responses is important with such children, but the teacher must be careful to give sufficient help through providing clues or through simplifying questions so that the student will be able to make a response. If she fails to do this, the whole procedure may backfire, and the student's anxiety about public response opportunities may increase rather than decrease.

In high SES schools (or more specifically, with students who are both competent and confident), the same techniques are optimal, but for somewhat different reasons. Where students are so eager to respond that mechanisms to minimize call outs and help insure equal opportunities become essential, patterned turns generally are superior to "random" turns in reading group. Also, attempts to get the student to improve his response can easily backfire in the early grade levels with such children, because the nature of the questions is such that the student usually either knows the answer or does not. As a result, if he fails to answer the question within a second or two, he probably is not going to be able to answer it, and he is unlikely to benefit from help (other than some extreme form of help which virtually gives him the answer), with the exception of phonics clues which sometimes will enable a child to sound out a word he is stuck on. The vast majority of the response opportunities at these grade levels involve short (usually one word) factual answers. Furthermore, the answers usually are such that the student either does or does not know them; seldom can they be reasoned out through logical processes.

This is because much of the factual information and basic skills being taught in the early grades is established by social convention rather than logical necessity. There is no reason (at least, none that can be coherently understood by a young child) why numbers and letters have the shapes that they do, why certain words are spelled the way they are spelled, why things are called by one particular name rather than another, etc. These and related matters are facts which must be committed to memory; they usually cannot be deduced through reasoning. Consequently, in contrast to higher grade levels, where it often is possible for a student to reason through to a conclusion about some complex matter because the steps involved in arriving at the answer form a chain of logical sequences, answering questions in the early grades usually is a case of "you know it or you don't." Under these circumstances, then, "improving" student responses is unlikely in most instances, so that seeking to bring about such "improvement" usually amounts to nothing more than pointless pumping.

Note that we have attributed most of the differences between our findings and those in the existing literature to differences in the ages of the children being studied. This point will be amplified in Chapter 12. First, however, we wish to discuss certain limitations inherent in the data we have presented which should be kept in mind by anyone who wishes to apply them to the classroom.

Cautions and Limitations

10

Before going on to discuss the implications of the data for teachers, we first will pause to remind readers of certain limitations in the study and to introduce certain others that should be kept in mind. One very important limitation was that only cognitive criteria were used: student learning gains on a standardized, norm-referenced achievement test. We believe that this criterion was particularly appropriate in the present study because the test had been in use for many years in the school system involved, but nevertheless it remains true that the test undoubtedly was not equally "fair" to all teachers because it did not equally measure the teaching goals that different teachers were striving for in their classroom instruction. That is, to the extent that one teacher spent more time teaching material that would help her classes do well on this test than another teacher did, the first teacher had an advantage over the second teacher. If this advantage was due to a difference in teaching goals rather than to greater efficiency on the part of the first teacher, it could be said legitimately that the test was relatively unfair or was less fair for the second teacher.

This problem is not unique to our study, of course. Every study that uses any criterion of teacher effectiveness will be using one that is differentially "fair" to different teachers depending upon how closely it reflects what the teachers actually tried to accomplish during the school year. Also, internal data from our project provided reasonable assurance that unfairness was not an important problem in the present study. The teachers were chosen on the basis of their consistent relative success in producing learning gains as measured by the tests used, and the data seemed to indicate rather clearly that the differences between the more versus the less successful teachers were due to differences in efficiency and thoroughness of teaching rather than in what they decided to teach. Thus, we personally are not particularly concerned about the fairness of the test as a measure of success in producing learning gains. However, at the same time, we must point out that the test *only* measured success in producing learning gains; we did not systematically measure teacher success in producing positive student attitudes or other affective goals.

We did make an attempt to measure affective variables in the students (attitudes toward the teacher), but the measurement instrument involved proved to be too difficult for too many of the children to use validly, so that we were unable to obtain usable data. Consequently, our information about the affective aspects of teaching is limited to the teacher responses to the interview and questionnaire items and to certain aspects of the observational data. Fortunately, this information is reasonably detailed, so that we do have a good picture of the affective aspects of each teacher's classroom. This is based on observation of teacher-student interaction by our observers, however, and does not include responses obtained directly from the students. This weakness is being remedied in a follow up study.

In any case, our process observation data were sufficient to counter the notion that the typical classroom is a dreary, frustrating place presided over by a discontented and hostile teacher. Our observers found most of the classrooms to be quite cheerful and pleasant, and most of the teachers to be warm and student oriented, regardless of their success in producing student learning gains.

However, it was true that certain negativistic teacher behaviors, particularly criticism for poor responses or seatwork, correlated positively with student learning gains, and it is reasonable to suppose that they would correlate negatively with student attitudes toward the teacher. This is not surprising, or at least it should not be, because numerous other studies have found that variables which correlate positively with cognitive gains often correlate negatively with affective gains, and vice versa. In fact, this seem to be the standard situation in studies conducted at the college level (Turner and Thompson, 1974).

Unfortunately, it appears that a certain degree of trade off between cognitive gains and the achievement of affective goals is likely to appear in most naturalistic teaching situations, so that, for some teaching behaviors at least, increases in behavior that will help the teacher achieve cognitive goals will at the same time impede progress toward affective goals, and vice versa. Of course, this introduces problems of value judgments concerning what are appropriate educational goals and what is appropriate teacher behavior. In any case, readers should remain aware that the correlations discussed in the present book all relate teacher characteristics to success in producing student learning gains (a purely cognitive goal), and that these gains were measured by a norm-referenced achievement test.

We already have stated this several times, but is is worth repeating: bear in mind that all of the data presented here are *correlational*. That is, they show that a teacher characteristic is associated, either linearly or nonlinearly, with student learning gains. In most cases, follow up experimental research probably will reveal that the relationship is *causal*, that the teacher characteristics cause relatively poor or good learning gains. However, so long as the relationships remain at the correlational level, and causality is not demonstrated through experiments that involve deliberate manipulation of the teacher behavior in question in order to see if it has the predicted effects, suggestions that the teacher characteristics cause the student outcomes must remain at the level of inferential hypotheses, not demonstrated facts. Our data show that the more successful teachers in our sample differed from the less successful teachers in certain systematic ways, but they do not by themselves demonstrate that these differences were the reasons for or the direct causes of their differential levels of success in producing student learning gains.

It is possible, and in fact probable, that some of the relationships between teacher characteristics and student learning gains are not directly causal. In such cases, the relationships are indirect and appear because the teacher characteristic involved is associated with another, more fundamental, characteristic, which is the real cause of student outcomes.

For example, we have suggested several interpretations as to why the use of patterned reading turns was positively correlated with student learning gains. Most of these interpretations involve attribution of causality to more wide ranging and fundamental teacher traits, of which the use of patterned reading turns is only a small part. Thus, an implication here, assuming that our interpretations are correct, is that a teacher who achieved the same basic results because she had the general characteristics considered to be important might get good learning gains even if she did not use patterned reading turns. Conversely, a teacher who used patterned reading turns but did so in isolation from all of the other factors considered to be important and related to the effects in question would not be expected to achieve very satisfactory results. Thus, it is possible (and in this case, we think, likely) that the use of patterned reading turns by itself is not especially important, and that the positive correlations for this teaching variable were obtained because the use of patterned reading turns was only a small part of a much larger pattern of teacher attitudes and behavior.

Complex relationships of this kind are possible for all of the teacher characteristics discussed in this book, so that it would be inappropriate to take a single specific finding in isolation from the other behaviors with which it was related and assume that it would have the same relationships to learning gains that it had in the context of the present study. With children of different ages or grade levels, different kinds of criteria, different contextual factors, or other differences from the present study, the relationships might not hold up.

This caution is doubly important when taken in combination with the reminder that a certain portion of the relationships we obtained may be spurious. That is, although they were technically statistically significant in our study, they might not exist in reality. Part of the problem was basic to the design of our study; we were studying over a thousand variables but using relatively small numbers of teachers. This procedure violates several of the assumptions underlying the use of statistics to determine probability values, so that the statistics concerning whether or not a particular relationship was "statistically significant" were not particularly meaningful in our study. Also, we used a probability value of .10 rather than the more strict and typical values of .05 or .01, thus increasing the likelihood of false positive findings (that is, data suggesting relationships when no relationship in fact exists). Furthermore, relatively few of the correlations or other relationships were extremely strong, tending to be more moderate or even weak and barely significant. Taken together, these data suggest that the danger of false positive findings in this study was particularly high, and that certain of the relationships reported here will not be replicated in subsequent studies.

Mitigating against this, however, is the fact that the study was replicated across two years, and that replication data therefore were available on the behavioral process data (not, however, on the interview or questionnaire data). We have taken this into account in writing the book, presenting only the main findings that replicated across two years and hung together to make good sense. Isolated findings that appeared for only one of the two years and had only borderline significance were ignored for the most part, on the assumption that they probably were spurious (chance) findings rather than findings reflecting real relationships.

Thus, we have attempted to compensate for the unusually high danger of false positives by remaining conservative in the number and kinds of findings reported in the book. Readers interested in seeing the full data should consult the detailed reports listed in Appendix C.

The self report data from the interviews and especially the questionnaires should be considered particularly suspect, because these data had unusually low rates of significant relationships, because self report data are open to numerous sources of bias, and because our analyses of the relationships between self report data and observational data on variables in common showed that teachers often were inaccurate in reporting their own classroom behavior. That is, what was observed in their classrooms did not closely match what they said they did on the questionnaires and interviews.

For example, few teachers were willing to state that they would tell a child that he was wrong when he had made a mistake. For some reason, the teachers believed that telling a child that he is wrong is likely to harm his self concept. However, classroom observations revealed that teachers virtually always informed a child that he was wrong when he gave a wrong answer (and that they did so quite appropriately, without overreacting in a negativistic way or doing anything else that might really damage self esteem). Thus, in this and certain other instances, the teachers' self report data showed signs of social desirability in their response patterns, with teachers apparently telling us what they felt they "should" say, even in situations where there was no good reason why they "should" say what they thought they were supposed to say.

Other teacher responses to the interviews and questionnaires indicated a certain amount of defensiveness and denial or rationalization in their responding. For example, most teachers believed that they praised much more often and criticized much less often than was actually the case. As mentioned repeatedly previously, most of these teachers were quite student oriented in their everyday classroom behavior, so that they had little or nothing to apologize for in regard to praise and criticism of their students. Nevertheless, most of them stated that they praised much more often than they really did and criticized much less often than they really did.

Numerous other discrepancies like these have led us to discount or at least question the self report data, and we have included in the book only the data that we feel reasonably confident about. Even so, readers should bear in mind that these are self report data which are automatically more suspect than behavioral data, and also that the findings concerning self report data are based on only one set of self report measures; there was no replication of this part of the study.

Although the study introduced some major methodological advances over previous work in process-product research, it had certain other limitations that affect the findings. One weakness was that context differences were controlled at only the grossest levels (morning observations vs. afternoon observations vs. reading group observations; teacher initiated vs. student initiated; public response opportunity situations vs. private contacts). We were unable to control for other potentially important context factors that might have made an important difference in the nature of the results (subject matter; beginnings vs. middles vs. ends of units; structural and spatial factors in the classrooms). The factors of curriculum differences and beginnings vs. middles vs. ends of units were crudely controlled by scheduling observations so that each teacher was observed periodically and at roughly similar times. This probably was reasonably effective the second year, but in the first year, when only four observations per teacher were made, it is likely that these contextual factors significantly affected our process data and therefore reduced the number of significant process-product relationships revealed.

Since we were working in naturalistic situations, there was no way that we could control for differences in classroom structure, in the physical condition or appearance of classrooms, or in student-teacher ratios. We did try to evaluate the relative importance of the last factor by rating the crowdedness of the classroom and certain other aspects of the physical situation. These data proved ambiguous, however. In the first year, there were sizeable negative correlations between ratings of classroom crowding and measures of student learning gains. However, the data from the second year revealed no significant relationships for classroom crowding. Fortunately, replication failures such as these, in which a measure that showed strong relationships the first year failed to reveal significant relationships the second year, were rare, but this was one of them. We tend to believe the second year data, partially because they were based on many more observations, and partially because studies of class size typically reveal it to be unrelated to learning gains, except in the most extreme situations (class sizes of only a few students). In any case, class size and the physical size and condition of the rooms in which the teachers taught were uncontrolled.

Finally, one of the most important weaknesses of the study was that we were unable to collect and record data on individual students, so that all of the process-product relationships reported were based on class means. We know that this is far from ideal, because much teacher behavior is directed at individual students rather than at the class as a whole (Good and Brophy, 1971). Furthermore, teachers often treat individual students differently, sometimes appropriately and sometimes not (Brophy and Good, 1974). These individualization differences were missed because we did not have data on individual students (data of this kind are being collected in a follow-up study).

Taken together, the lack of controls for important contextual differences and the lack of data on individual students were somewhat serious limitations on the potential of the study for revealing significant relationships. It now is quite clear that successful teaching is not so much a matter of mastering and applying a relatively small set of basic skills as it is a matter of mastering and applying a very large repertoire of specific skills. Part of this teaching ability is the ability to recognize what skills are appropriate at a given moment for use with a given student, and this aspect of teaching effectiveness was not systematically studied in the present research. This point will be discussed at greater length in Chapter 12.

Related Findings From Other Observers

11

In this chapter, we will briefly review the findings of others who have looked at the relationships between teacher characteristics and student learning in the early elementary grades. We make no attempt to cover the teacher effectiveness literature comprehensively here. Excellent recent reviews already are available (Dunkin and Biddle, 1974; Rosenshine and Furst, 1973). Our main purpose in this chapter is to show that our findings mostly reinforce or at least are compatible with other *research*, even though they often contradict certain popular *theories*.

Dunkin and Biddle (1974), in their review of the teacher effectiveness literature, noted that most theorists and even some researchers have very strong commitments to particular ideas, and that these commitments tend to shape their perceptions and even their interpretations of data. Furthermore, such commitments often cause textbook writers to strongly advocate certain ideas, even when there are no research data to support them. The result is that many teachers develop strong commitments to these ideas, independently of research data. This has happened in several areas.

We would like to point out a second problem: writers with strong commitments tend to think of good teaching as mastery and practice of their own pet methods. Even where research data support these methods, we think that this is not the way to conceptualize good teaching. Teaching in general, and good teaching in particular, is *not* simply a matter of using a few "crucial" techniques regularly. Instead, it is a matter of mastering and orchestrating a large number of principles, using them as appropriate to specific situations.

In any case, some of our data may be surprising to those who have been committed to certain ideas or who were under the impression that these ideas were backed by research. However, a survey of the existing research shows that most of it is quite compatible with our own findings.

Attitudes and Role Definitions

The notion that it is important for a teacher to take personal responsibility for student learning, and to accept the fact that successful teaching requires time and hard work, is hardly new. Just about everyone who has investigated teacher effectiveness has discovered that qualities like these are important. Some of the less obvious aspects of attitudes and role definitions found to be important in this study also have been supported in other research. For example, Faunce (1970) studied the characteristics and attitudes of teachers of disadvantaged children. The teachers were classified as effective and ineffective. The more effective teachers, like the more effective teachers of disadvantaged children in our study, had realistic rather than romanticized notions of children. They recognized that physical and material deprivation are real problems, and that not all children have equal opportunities because of differences in native ability, family resources, and environmental factors. However, they did not let these facts interfere with their ability to teach the children effectively without rejecting them or stereotyping them.

The variables of determination and thoroughness appeared in a study by Siegel and Rosenshine (1972). Here, teachers who were most successful in teaching disadvantaged children were more likely than other teachers to require correct responses from students (rather than give the answer or move on to someone else), to correct student mistakes by reviewing the entire task and checking again later to make sure that the student understood, and to carefully implement the curriculum as instructed (the curriculum was specially prepared for use with disadvantaged children).

Classroom Management

Much has been said elsewhere in the book about other findings concerning classroom management. Probably the most important point to bear in mind is that almost all surveys of teacher effectiveness report that classroom management skills are of primary importance in determining teaching success, whether it is measured by student learning or by ratings. Thus, management skills are crucial and fundamental. A teacher who is grossly inadequate in classroom management skills is probably not going to accomplish much.

A second major point to emphasize is that our data strongly support the findings of Kounin (1970), as well as the general ideas which underlie behavior modification. That is, the key to successful classroom management is prevention of problems before they start, not knowing how to deal with problems after they have begun. We also strongly confirmed the additional findings of Kounin, that the best way to accomplish this is to have a variety of appropriate assignments prepared, so that students not presently involved in a lesson will have interesting and appropriate work to do at their seats. If they do, they will tend to stay involved in productive and appropriate activities. If they do not, they will tend to cause disruption.

Matching Demands to Student Abilities

The general principle of matching cognitive demands to the student's present knowledge and abilities is one that few would argue with, although it is honored more in theory than in practice. Our data certainly indicate that the teacher must individualize, based on diagnoses and evaluations of students, regardless of the specific curriculum being taught. Also, other investigators have turned up findings mutually supportive of many of those reported in the present study.

For example, Cronbach (1967) found that students high in achievement motivation and low in anxiety (corresponding roughly to the high SES students in our study) reacted positively to criticism for poor work. In contrast, students with low motivation and high anxiety (corresponding roughly to the low SES students in our study) responded poorly to criticism but positively to praise and encouragement. Cronbach concluded that students with low achievement motivation and high anxiety do best when their teacher defines short term goals, gives maximum explanations and guidance, and provides frequent feedback at short intervals. All of these findings and comments are quite compatible with our findings.

Dunkin and Biddle (1974), reviewing a large volume of theory and research on level of classroom discourse (concrete to abstract, simple to complex, etc.), note that theorists usually recommend higher levels of discourse for higher achievement. However, the data do not support these theories, providing either mixed findings or negative findings. In particular, the data on young children provide the most striking negative findings.

For example, Ragosta, Soar, Soar, and Stebbins (1971) found, unsurprisingly, that highly focused and concrete tasks were related to pupil growth in simple and concrete skills. However, they also found that teacher emphasis on these "low level" tasks and skills maximized pupil growth on more abstract and complex skills. The teachers who were more successful teaching simple skills also were more successful teaching complex skills. Also, they did it through such behaviors as giving and receiving information, asking simple, relatively easy questions, asking questions that were narrow rather than broad in scope, and teaching lessons that were highly focused. These methods are similar to those that Cronbach had recommended for students low in achievement motivation and high in anxiety, and they also clearly were direct rather than indirect methods. Nevertheless, such methods maximized pupil learning of complex as well as simple skills.

Wright and Nuthall (1970) found that closed questions (similar to product questions in our study) were positively related to achievement by third graders, while open questions (similar to process questions in our study) were slightly negatively related to student learning. They were surprised by these findings, although they fit our data nicely. Also, Wright and Nuthall did not find the expected positive relationships between student talk and learning or between high level, complex teacher feedback and learning. They did find a positive relationship for calling on several students rather than restricting interaction to only a few, a finding that seems compatible with our data concerning patterned turns.

Stallings (1974), in a review of the evaluation data for Project Follow Through, reported that higher reading and math scores in both first and third grades were achieved by teachers working with highly structured models. These models featured carefully prepared lessons, behavioral objectives, short steps and smooth pacing, and a strong emphasis on continual evaluation and reteaching to make sure that all of the children mastered the material. All of these teaching techniques are compatible with what was found effective here. In contrast, Follow Through models which emphasized discovery learning, minimized teacher directiveness, and/or maximized pupil-to-pupil interaction were the least effective, apparently because the children were not ready for them yet.

Soar and Soar (1974), summarizing data accumulated across several studies of teaching and learning in the early grades, concluded that teaching involves the orchestration of behaviors which are mostly related curvilinearly to student outcomes, that a majority of significant correlations between teaching process measures and student outcome measures will be negative ones, and that overly difficult questions or problems will be negatively associated with learning gains. These all are highly compatible with the findings from the present study.

Finally, Hambleton (1974), after reviewing the major individualized learning programs, concluded that difficulty level was curvilinearly related to success. Apparently, behavioral objectives which set ideal mastery levels at 80 to 85 percent produced the best results. Higher levels get better congnitive results but reduced affect (the students learn more but enjoy it less) while lower levels do not allow sufficient mastery for the students to truly learn the material. These data are quite compatible with those in the present study, particularly when taken in conjunction with the data of Crawford (1975). That is, material should be easy when the student will be expected to work alone, as in individualized learning programs, but should be somewhat more difficult when the teacher is available to present it and to correct errors. Hambleton also noted that it is better to err on the side of giving the student extra practice on something he has already mastered than to misdiagnose him as having mastered it and thus to fail to give him the practice he needs. In short, over-teaching is better than under-teaching.

Diagnosis and Evaluation

Many data suggest that teachers who remain aware of the fact that tests are merely tools to provide information and not devices for labeling or stereotyping students are more successful teachers. For a detailed review of studies concerning teacher reactions to test data, and for illustrations of how rigid and inappropriate teacher expectations for student achievement can lead to undesirable self-fulfilling prophecy effects, see Brophy and Good (1974).

St. John (1971) reported interesting findings concerning the use of test data in a study of 36 teachers working in integrated classrooms with black and white students.The teachers who were more successful with black students were rated highly on such traits as kindliness, adaptability, and optimism. Also, these teachers did *not* consider test scores to be reliable indicators of pupil ability. The attitudes of these teachers toward standardized tests were similar to those of the successful low SES teachers in our study.

Public Response Opportunities

Dunkin and Biddle (1974) characterize the concept of "indirect teaching" as one which has been advocated overly strongly by individuals committed to it. They note that the research data supporting it are mixed, and that few studies control for student attributes such as I.Q. or social class. This is important, because many studies have revealed that teachers tend to be more indirect toward brighter and better motivated students. However, this may be a student effect on teachers, rather than the opposite.

In any case, it seems clear from the available data that indirect teaching is not appropriate for young children in the early elementary grades. Flanders himself notes this (Flanders, 1970). In reviewing studies related to indirect teaching, he comments that the data supporting the concept are weakest for studies conducted in the early grades. Referring to earlier work by Soar, he concludes that indirect teaching probably is related curvilinearly to student learning, so that the most indirect teachers probably will be less successful than those who have a more optimal level of indirectness. Soar had found indirect teaching to be related curvilinearly to achievement gains, with the optimal level being lower for concrete tasks than for abstract tasks. These findings closely parallel our own, and they provide more support for our interpretations of our findings.

Numerous other studies also have found that verbal participation by pupils is relatively unimportant, and that teacher instruction followed by pupil opportunity to practice and get corrective feedback is relatively more important, in the early grades. For example, Francis (1975) found that first-, third-, and sixth-grade students acquired both simple and *complex* concepts when taught through lecture methods more quickly and easily than when taught with discovery methods. The superiority of students taught with lecture methods was higher not only on memory tests but also on transfer tests, a finding that sharply contradicts one of the more common assumptions underlying the concept of discovery learning.

Hughes (1973) found that manipulations of the order in which students were called on to respond and of the frequencies with which they were asked questions did not affect student learning in seventh grade science lessons. Thus, the sheer frequency with which a pupil participated in public response opportunities was relatively unimportant. However, the nature of teacher response to such pupil participations was important. Pupils who were given complete feedback about the correctness or incorrectness of their answers, and who also were praised or reproved according to the situation, showed better achievement than pupils who received minimal responses from the teachers.

Hughes' data concerning teacher reactions to student answers closely parallel our own. His findings that frequency of student participation and method of calling on students (random vs. deliberately patterned) did not make a difference conflicts with ours. However, his students were seventh graders who were more able to learn from listening to other students and probably less in need of personal interaction with the teacher, as compared to the students in our study.

Meissner (1975) studied learning by second and fourth grade disadvantaged black children. She found that the children possessed sufficiently well developed receptive language to enable them to benefit from instruction from others, but that their expressive language was not yet developed well enough to make them effective in *communicating* information. One conclusion she drew was that pupil-to-pupil communication was an inefficient and ineffective mechanism for learning in the early elementary grades, particularly for disadvantaged children.

In summary, the concept of indirect teaching, or more broadly, the idea of teaching primarily through verbal discussion and frequent pupil-to-pupil interaction, receives little support in studies conducted at the early elementary grades. Apparently, children of this age, especially disadvantaged children, are not yet cognitively or linguistically ready to respond optimally to this approach to teaching. Furthermore, they seem to need much individualized contact with the teacher, so that their assignments can be monitored closely and so that they can receive whatever corrective feedback they need. In summary, public response opportunities and the concept of indirect teaching refer to teaching conducted primarily through verbal discourse, and this is not the kind of teaching that is (or should be) conducted in the early elementary grades.

Motivation and Incentives

Dunkin and Biddle (1974), after reviewing a large number of studies, concluded that a general climate of acceptance and warmth towards students is more important than specific praise from the teacher. Our findings support their general conclusion. They also note that the data on criticism are mixed, probably in part because many investigators have failed to distinguish between intense personal criticism and simple negative feedback that tells the student that he is wrong without criticizing him personally. Our findings are compatible with this conclusion, too, and also with the general finding of an interaction between the effectiveness of praise and criticism and certain student attributes. For example, as mentioned earlier, St. John (1971) found that warmer and more student-oriented teachers were more successful in producing achievement among disadvantaged black students. More generally, several studies have found that teachers who are warm and student oriented tend to be the most successful when working with students who lack confidence, are anxious about school, and/or are members of rejected minority groups (Brophy and Good, 1974).

Data from child development and experimental psychology suggest similar conclusions. Thompson and Hunnicut (1944) found that introverts responded better to praise, while extroverts responded better to criticism. Van de Riet (1964) found that praise was more effective with normally achieving children, but that criticism was more effective with underachievers (students who were not working as hard or carefully as they could, and thus were not achieving as much as they were capable of achieving). French (1958) found that learners with high achievement motivation did better when teachers gave them task relevant feedback, including criticism. In contrast, those with high affiliation needs (students more interested in pleasing the teacher and being liked than in achieving) worked better when the teacher gave them more personalized feedback and encouragement.

Thus, our conclusion that teacher verbal praise is not of paramount importance in its own right draws support from several sources, although the accompanying conclusion that praise does have some importance and should be used appropriately also holds up. So does our finding that criticism appears appropriate for high ability students who give answers or turn in work that is clearly below their capabilities. However, it should be kept in mind that such criticism should be confined to the poor work, and should not be part of a more general pattern of rejection and negativism.

The basic reasons for these findings probably are positive expectations and encouragement rather than praise and criticism. Praise which is genuine and encouraging to the student probably is positively motivating, while praise that is hollow or perfunctory might do more harm than good. Similarly, although overly strong or unjustified criticism probably would be destructive, chiding a student for doing work well below his capacities probably will be successful not only in getting him to improve his work but also in communicating positive expectations. Thus, paradoxically, under the right circumstances, criticism can foster positive student self concepts.

"Unexpected" Findings

Even some of the findings that were listed as "unexpected"

are supported by the findings of other investigators. The key here probably lies in the criterion of effectiveness. Teacher attributes such as warmth, praise, enthusiasm, and indirectness have been supported in numerous studies, but most of these have used affective rather than achievement criteria in judging teacher effectiveness. Since our data have been confined to the relationships between teacher characteristics and student learning gains, perhaps it should not be so surprising that positive relationships involving these teacher affective characteristics were not found.

Other important keys are the ages of the students and the nature of teaching and learning in the early elementary grades. Again, numerous studies have supported the importance of variables such as teacher questioning strategies, the use of advance organizers, and other aspects of verbal discourse in the classroom. However, as pointed out above, verbal discourse occupies a relatively small part of the day in the typical classroom in the early elementary grades (appropriately so, apparently). It becomes more important later when the children master basic skills and begin to apply them. In any case, given that verbal discourse is not particularly important in the early grades, it follows that variables related to successful verbal discourse would not be very important, either.

Conclusions
and Implications
for Teaching

12

So far, we have discussed the basic design of our research, presented the highlights of the findings, discussed certain limitations and cautions that should be kept in mind by readers who are interested in applying the data to the classroom, and discussed related findings by other investigators. We now will discuss what we see as some of the major implications of the study. This necessarily will involve jumping ahead and treating these correlational findings as if they were causal findings (that is, acting as if correlated teacher characteristics *caused* student outcomes). As noted in Chapter 10, this is a reasonable *assumption* for most of our findings, but it remains an assumption. Correlation does not indicate causality.

With this caution in mind, let us consider what our data might mean. First, the many contradictions between our findings and those of previous researchers working at higher grade levels, coupled with the fact that the discrepancies all are rather easily related to considerations of student age and the nature of the teaching-learning process at different grade levels, seems to indicate that teaching in the early elementary grades (and presumably also in preschool) is fundamentally different in many ways from teaching at the higher grades. This means not only that the teaching of young children should be studied in its own right and conceptualized and discussed differently, but, if you carry this reasoning to its logical conclusion, that teachers intending to teach very young children in the early elementary grades should be given specific and prescriptive training which differs from that given to teachers intending to work at higher grade levels.

Traditionally, teacher education programs have distinguished only between the elementary and the secondary levels, with preschool being added more recently as a third level. Our data, as well as those of several other investigators (notably Soar, 1972), suggest that different teacher education arrangements might be more optimal. One might be to subdivide elementary teachers into those intending to teach in the first three grades and those intending to teach at higher grades. Another possibility would be to combine preschool teacher preparation with the preparation of teachers for the first three grades, and then make an additional separation somewhere later along the line between teachers of children in middle childhood vs. teachers working with adolescents.

In any case, it seems quite clear that teachers working with preoperational children and concentrating on teaching the fundamentals of reading, writing, and arithmetic face a task which is different in many ways from the task facing teachers who are working with older students and teaching highly conceptual material through primarily verbal methods. The former type of teaching requires much teacher structured presentation of new material, followed closely by opportunities for the children to practice the new skill or concept and to get immediate corrective feedback. Most of the emphasis is on acquisition of these basic skills and practice of them to the point of overlearning. In contrast, the emphasis in later grades is on using these basic skills for the more applied purposes of learning conceptual content in the traditional curriculum areas. The nature of the learner and the nature of the teaching-learning situation are so different that separate teacher training seems to be in order.

The Nature of Teaching

A second major implication from this study, mentioned briefly at the end of Chapter 10, is that *effective teaching is not simply a matter of implementing a small number of "basic" teaching skills. Instead, effective teaching requires the ability to implement a very large number of diagnostic, instructional, managerial, and therapeutic skills, tailoring behavior in specific contexts and situations to the specific needs of the moment.* Effective teachers not only must be able to do a large number of things; they also must be able to recognize which of the many things they know how to do applies at a given moment and be able to follow through by performing the behavior effectively. In short, effective teaching involves **orchestration** of a large number of factors, continually shifting teaching behavior to respond to continually shifting needs.

With benefit of hindsight, this conclusion seems rather obvious, even trite. Nevertheless, educational researchers and textbooks writers often act as if they were unaware of it, especially if they are strong advocates of particular teaching styles or techniques. Exceptions like Hunt and Ausubel have continually pointed out the need to match instruction to the learner's present levels of achievement and interest, and concepts such as individualization, diagnostic teaching, prescriptive teaching, and individually prescribed instruction, among others, do seem to recognize this principle at least implicitly.

However, most teacher education textbooks give it lip service at best, and instead present a fairly narrow model of what the authors consider to be "good" teaching. More often than not, their formulas involve mastery of a small number of particular characteristics or teaching behaviors that *presumably* will work with *all* students in *any* circumstances. Upon reflection, this is easily seen as obvious nonsense. Nevertheless, it is common, perhaps even typical.

This is unfortunate, because it means that teachers who take seriously what they have been taught in education courses advocating a narrow model will not be maximally effective, and some will be grossly ineffective. For example, teachers who seriously tried to implement an approach that featured concepts such as indirect teaching, discovery learning, independent learning, avoidance of structured lessons, and the like, probably would be hopelessly ineffective if they were working with children in the early elementary grades, particularly in low SES schools.

Developmental Considerations

The above example introduces another important point which combines the two main points discussed in this chapter so far: There appear to be systematic interactions between the ages and levels of cognitive development of children and the kinds of teaching that are optimal for them. Younger and less cognitively developed children seem to require more teacher structuring, smaller and more redundant steps in the learning process, more opportunities to practice and get corrective feedback, more attention to basic skills and factual knowledge, and the like. As they get older and/or more cognitively developed, they can begin to benefit increasingly from more indirect teaching, more verbal teaching, more opportunities for choice of assignments and independent work, more opportunities for group work and other student-to-student interaction, more challenging and faster paced instructional sequences, and the like.

This means, among other things, that: optimal teaching behavior in the lower grades will differ from optimal teaching behavior in higher grades; optimal teaching within a given grade will differ by the SES level of the school in communities where schools are segregated along SES lines (as they usually are); and, even within individual classrooms, optimal teaching behavior will differ for different students depending upon their levels of cognitive development and achievement. Effective teachers will be aware of these differences and will tailor their teaching to each specific student's individual needs. Teachers who fail to do this and instead attempt to teach the whole class with a single method will fail with some of their less competent students, because they move too fast and expect too much, and also will be relatively unsuccessful (compared to what they could have accomplished) with some of their most competent students, because they will be providing insufficient variety and challenge.

Role Definitions and Expectations

Running throughout our data are indications that teachers' role definitions for themselves and expectations for their students are among the most fundamental teacher characteristics associated with teaching success. The most effective teachers appeared to have realistic and correct expectations concerning their students, being neither gushingly romantic nor cynically discouraged. They recognized real differences between students' present capacities and achievement levels, but they use this information to plan learning experiences that will optimally assist students in moving forward, not merely to label the students or to provide excuses for failing to teach them properly.

Effective teachers also had realistic and appropriate role definitions. That is, they recognized and accepted the fundamental notion that their primary responsibility as teachers is to *teach*. This meant they they took personal responsibility for their students' learning and were prepared to do whatever turned out to be necessary to insure that such learning occurred. They viewed failure as feedback telling them that new or different approaches were required, not as indications that the student could not learn. Thus, they spent little time rationalizing learning failures, responding instead with renewed effort to circumvent the problem through alternative approaches.

Also, although effective teachers typically were affectionate and student oriented, they tended to place the personal relationship aspects of teaching secondary to the instructional aspects. Thus, while they enjoyed their work and liked children, they did not have gushy or romanticized images of children and did not seem to need or want strong emotional relationships with their students. In short, they operated as professionals who saw their role as providing the students with what the students needed, in contrast to attempting to use relationships with students to satisfy their own emotional needs (the impression that our observers gathered after observing teachers who had an overblown, romanticized view of the young child).

Proactive Structuring of the Learning Environment

Effective teachers not only felt themselves to be in control of the situation and defined their role as one of doing whatever was necessary in order to meet their goals; they followed through with appropriate behavior. Much of the behavior that distinguished the most effective teachers from the less effective ones was behavior that could be called "proactive." That is, it was behavior initiated by the teachers themselves, often prior to the beginning of the school year or the beginning of a particular school day. This is in contrast to reactive behavior that teachers show in situations when students do something that forces them to make some kind of immediate reactive response.

Proactive behavior included such things as obtaining, storing, and preparing for use when needed special materials that are useful in helping a child who is having difficulty with a particular concept; organizing the physical space in the classroom for maximum efficiency and effective group living; planning monitor systems and other mechanisms for seeing that the daily housekeeping routines of the classroom get accomplished "automatically" and with minimum disruption; planning mechanisms and developing the necessary materials to set up a system to enable children who need help with their seatwork to get it without interrupting the teacher and to insure that children who finish their seatwork have some interesting and useful activity to do; planning classroom rules and presenting them effectively to the children; developing tests and observational devices to gather prescriptive and diagnostic information on student progress; initiating and maintaining cooperative relationships with parents; and, in general, anticipating and being prepared for whatever contingencies might occur, rather than having to react to them without being properly prepared.

We are quite aware that this concept of the effective teacher involves considerable dedication and professionalism. At first glance, it might seem extremely difficult, beyond the reach of most individuals. To a degree, we would agree with this assessment; teaching is not for people who are looking for a soft job. On the other hand, we suspect that learning to be an effective teacher is not quite so difficult as it might seem at first. Most of the specific behaviors involved are not especially difficult to perform in themselves; the most difficult part would appear to be learning to orchestrate them properly, treating one student one way in one situation and another student a different way in a different situation, according to situational demands.

We believe that well adjusted college students who have appropriate role definitions of what teaching involves, who want to become good teachers, and who apply themselves appropriately, can acquire the skills that will make them consistently effective. However, it will be important for such persons to sharpen their observational skills and approach the task with what we have called a proactive orientation.

At the moment, teaching is partly an art, because of the limited knowledge base relating teacher behavior to student outcomes. Hopefully, teaching will evolve into an applied science as this knowledge base increases, so that successful teachers will operate like successful doctors or lawyers, using diagnostic skills to determine what principles apply to a particular situation and then following up with problem solving skills that will enable them to reach their goals.

The Need for Information About Effective Teaching Behavior

The analogy between teaching and law, medicine, and other professions raises an important point relevant to recent controversial issues. In our opinion, much time and energy has been wasted misapplying accountability devices to teachers. The accountability notion is a good one in theory, and hopefully at some point it will be operationalized appropriately in practice. However, at present it is not possible to operationalize it appropriately in practice, despite the claims of its proponents.

The basic reason for this is that the requisite knowledge base does not exist. Teachers take a national teaching examination when they graduate from college, but this examination repeatedly has been shown to be unrelated to any subsequent measure of teacher behavior or teacher effectiveness. With the benefit of hindsight, we can see that this finding should not be surprising, because the teaching exam tests the teacher's ability to show mastery of the content of teacher education textbooks, and, as we have frequently noted, the teaching behaviors propounded in these textbooks rarely are backed by empirical data.

Instead, they reflect present fads and/or the pet biases of their authors. Many of them are demonstrably incorrect, and even those which do appear to have general validity must be qualified in certain contexts or restricted in the range of students or situations to which they apply. Thus, the knowledge base that would be required to make teaching truly an applied science does not yet exist, and, in contrast to the qualifying procedures used in other professions, teaching presently is not amenable to a qualifying procedure or accountability device capable of assessing teaching skills validly.

Aware of the uselessness of the national teacher's examination and of other pencil and paper tests purporting to measure teacher effectiveness, educators involved in the accountability movement lately have begun to look into the feasibility of process and product measures as accountability devices. However, our data strongly indicate that neither of these data sets will suffice, at least for the present. As far as product data go, we already know that teacher behavior that maximizes progress toward cognitive goals often reduces progress toward other goals, and that most teachers are not consistent from one year to the next in their relative success, regardless of what criterion is used. Thus, the use of product criteria, which sounds very good in theory, is inappropriate and unfair in practice. Until there is some agreement about goals, and until teachers begin to show some consistency from one year to the next in their relative success in achieving goals, product criteria are not going to be very useful as accountability devices.

The same is true of process measures. Some advocates of particular process measures simply *assume* that teachers who behave in a certain way are good teachers, and consequently that these process behaviors can be used as criteria of teaching effectiveness, even though data relating these behaviors to student outcomes do not exist or even conflict with the theory. This obviously is ridiculous, but nevertheless teachers have been and still are being rewarded or punished because they did or did not show particular behaviors that their supervisors thought were important. Judging teacher effectiveness on the basis of observed behavior ultimately might be feasible, but not until the required knowledge base has been built up.

Developing Knowledge vs. Evaluating

This brings us to the main point we wish to make in this section: researchers, administrators, and others concerned with the measurement of teacher effectiveness should concentrate their efforts on discovering cause and effect relationships that will help build up a knowledge base concerning *effective teaching*. This is in contrast to activities designed to discover the characteristics of an *effective teacher*. As with any other profession that is an applied science, teaching is in need of a knowledge base to specify relationships between teacher behavior and student outcomes, including appropriate qualifications and elaborations which take into account situational context differences. If and when a sufficient knowledge base of this sort is developed, we can expect teaching to evolve more clearly into an applied science, teachers to become more consistent in their process behavior and in their product outcomes, and teaching effectiveness to be accessible to valid measurement. Not before.

Analogies with other professions may help illustrate both what kind of knowledge is needed and why the present search for effective teachers is self-defeating. First, consider the legal profession. If we applied a simple minded accountability approach to lawyers, we would reward them according to the percentage of cases that they won. However, all lawyers and most others realize that this would be a grossly inappropriate and unfair way to proceed. If "winning" is defined as obtaining a conviction (for a prosecuting lawyer) or obtaining acquittal (for a defense lawyer), lawyers' "batting averages" will be seriously distorted by the nature of the cases that they take.

In many cases, conviction or acquittal (depending upon the case) is virtually impossible because the facts are so clear cut and unchallenged that certain aspects of the outcome of the case are completely predictable in advance and known to all concerned. There is nothing that the lawyers on either side of the case can do about these factors. Consequently, their performance in the case will have to be judged by their skill in handling those aspects of the case that are ambiguous and open to argument and legal manuevering. In judging a fellow lawyer's handling of a particular case, lawyers would judge the degree to which he had gotten the best that could have been expected for his client, not simply whether he "won" or "lost."

The same is true in medicine and dentistry. Medical doctors are not judged on the basis of how long their patients live, and dentists are not judged on the basis of whether they saved a tooth vs. pulled it. Instead, like lawyers, these professionals are judged by the degree to which their handling of particular cases is appropriate and successful in accomplishing as much as can be expected under the circumstances. In summary, in professions that involve applied science based on a sound knowledge base, the knowledge base consists of information about the relationships between certain situations, certain professional behaviors, and certain expected outcomes; it is not simply a list of traits that "effective" professionals in the field are supposed to have.

While it would be possible to compute a "batting average" type of accountability score for these professionals, no one suggests doing it for the very good reason that it would be more confusing than helpful. For example, a doctor with an effectiveness score of 80% is not necessarily more useful to you than a doctor with an effectiveness score of 70%, particularly if you have a broken finger and the first doctor is a brain surgeon while the second one is a general practitioner. Thus, even if it were possible to scale professionals with general indexes representing the percentage of times that they handled specific problems with maximum efficiency or effectiveness, this general index would have relatively limited usefulness (and would probably be redundant because it would only certify with numbers what everybody already knew anyway).

In summary, then, we think that it is time for educators to abandon concepts of teaching based on the idea that successful teachers are those who have mastered a few techniques or who have acquired a few specific characteristics, and that it is time to abandon attempts to identify the characteristics of effective teachers when it is assumed implicitly that effectiveness will be indicated by the presence of certain "key" characteristics. Instead, attention should be turned to the development of a knowledge base linking specific situations (types of students, context factors, and teaching goals) with specific teacher behaviors and specific student outcomes. Ultimately, this will lead not only to more effective teaching, but also to a more appropriate conceptualization of teaching: the orchestration of specific behavior to meet the requirements of specific situations.

Teacher Selection Procedures

Appendix A

The design, data collection, and data analysis phases of the study took more than four years to complete, and they involved many innovations and many complex procedures. Consequently, everything cannot be discussed in great detail here, although the basic information needed to understand the study will be provided. Readers interested in detailed technical discussion of the design aspects of the study and/or in detailed tabular presentation of the results should consult the references listed in Appendix C.

The Research Setting

The teachers included in the study were selected from a larger sample of 165 teachers which included all of the second and third grade teachers in the Austin Independent School District who had been teaching at their respective grade levels for four or more consecutive years. The school district was chosen because: it was geographically convenient; it was large enough to include sufficient numbers of teachers for study; it had on file the needed records concerning student learning; and it was interested in and willing to cooperate with the study. Thus, the teacher sample was partly a sample of convenience, chosen because it was handy, and partly a sample of choice, selected because it had certain attributes that the study required.

So far as is known, the Austin school district is representative of city school districts in the country generally. The schools, teachers, and curricula seem typical in most respects, particularly for the Southwest. The student population is about 70% Anglo, 17% Mexican-American, and 13% Black, which is representative of the general population of the Southwest, where it is located. It differs from school districts in the other parts of the country primarily in that it contains very few members of European-American ethnic minority groups. Due to *de facto* segregation and the neighborhood school concept, the majority of the elementary schools in the district contain a preponderance of students of one of the three primary racial/ethnic groups.

Thus, except for differences in the specific white ethnic groups involved, the district seems representative of others serving small and medium sized cities. School desegregation efforts have included a teacher crossover plan, which placed more black teachers in white schools and more white teachers in black schools, and partial desegregation of student populations through busing. However, only the teacher crossover plan affected the schools involved in this study. Busing of students for desegregation purposes was limited to the junior high and high schools. Furthermore, the teacher crossover plan affected only a small percentage of teachers, so that most teachers in the district as a whole, and in this study in particular, had been teaching at the school at which they were presently teaching for some time.

The study could have been conducted at any grade

levels, but the second and third grades were chosen for a combination of practical and personal preference reasons. The practical reasons centered around the problem of finding appropriate criteria of teacher effectiveness and identifying samples of teachers who showed consistency on these criteria. This proved to be difficult at the junior high and high school level because of curriculum changes, shifts and disagreements about priorities concerning school objectives (and consequently, teacher effectiveness), and the new problems and adjustments facing everyone when school busing was instituted. Under the circumstances, even determining what effective teaching was, let alone designing a study to investigate it systematically, would have been difficult.

Thus, practical considerations pointed to the elementary schools. Happily, so did matters of personal preference. Our backgrounds and interests had centered on child development and early education (preschool and early primary grades), and our own children were in these age ranges at the time. Thus, we were especially interested in problems concerning teaching young children effectively.

Another consideration was the teacher's probable impact. An elementary teacher who works with the same class of children all day long for an entire school year seems likely to have a greater impact on students than a junior high or high school teacher who works with a given class for only about an hour a day, and sometimes only for one semester.

Also, it seemed likely that a teacher working with children in the early grades, who are still relatively young and presumably more adult oriented and malleable, should have a greater effect on them than a teacher working with older students, who presumably are less open to influence because they have had several more years of unique development in response to their unique environments. Compared to older children, younger children are less well developed and consequently more open to environmental influences, particularly to sustained and systematic influences such as those provided by a teacher over the course of an entire school year.

Taken together, these considerations led us to select for the study teachers who were working in self-contained classrooms in the early elementary grades. First grade teachers were eliminated from consideration for reasons to be described in the following section, so that second and third grade teachers were selected. The study was confined to these two grades for financial reasons. Teachers working in self-contained classrooms were selected because teacher effectiveness was to be determined by student outcomes, and thus it was essential that the progress of a given group of students could be attributed to the efforts of a particular teacher. This was not possible in team teaching situations where two or more teachers shared responsibility for a large group of students, since there is no way to determine what portion of a given student's progress is attributable to the efforts of a given teacher. Thus, teachers working in team teaching situations were excluded, and the study was confined to self-contained classrooms.

Teacher Effectiveness Criteria

Because subjective ratings by principals, supervisors, or curriculum experts are notoriously unreliable, we felt that it was essential to operationally define teacher effectiveness by some more reliable and objective method. The criterion we chose was *teacher success in producing student learning gains on standardized achievement tests*. This decision gave the study several important strengths, as well as some weaknesses, which will be discussed below. In any case, readers should bear in mind that the term "teacher effectiveness" and the term "effective teaching" as used in this book usually refer *only* to teacher success in producing student learning gains on standardized tests. Although most writers would agree that this is an important component of effective teaching, few would agree that it is the only one, and many would say that it is not even the most important one. Thus, readers should bear in mind what it does and does not mean.

As mentioned above, one of our reasons for wanting to work at the early elementary grades rather than at higher grades was the greater agreement about criteria of teacher effectiveness. That is, most writers agree that success in teaching students the fundamental tool skills traditionally taught in the early grades is an important, if not the most important, aspect of the teacher's role. Teaching other content such as social studies or racial/ethnic history also is thought to be important by many. So are aspects of socialization such as promoting moral development and social skills. Nevertheless, there is fairly general agreement that the fundamental tool skills of language arts and mathematics form the heart of the early elementary school curriculum and define the teacher's primary areas of responsibility.

There is much less agreement at later grades, where many observers place relatively more emphasis on the affective side of teaching relative to the cognitive side. For example, which of the following should be the primary goal of a high school English teacher?

Reading Comprehension

Writing and Composition Skills

Sentence Analysis and Grammatical Construction

Expressing Thoughts with Creativity and Originality
Familiarity with the "Classics"

Sampling the Wide Range of Literature to "Find Out What You Like"

Ability to Analyze Plot, Characterization, and other Literary Features

Being Able to Apply What One Reads to One's Personal Life

This is only a partial listing of some of the important goals that high school English teachers pursue. Even so, it is clear that a given teacher could not place equal attention and emphasis on all of these goals, and that there will be much disagreement among teachers, students, and the public at large concerning which goals are more important than others. The same kinds of problems exist, but to a much lesser degree, in the early elementary grades. Thus, equating effective teaching with the ability to produce learning gains on standardized tests of student achievement of fundamental tool skills in language arts and mathematics in the early grades seemed more likely to be acceptable to a larger number of people than equating teaching effectiveness with student content mastery at the higher grade levels would be.

The Test Data

Fortunately, student progress in mastering skills can be measured with objective tests. However, the criterion problem isn't solved simply by deciding to evaluate teachers according to their students' test scores. First, the tests must be *valid*. That is, they must appropriately measure what the teachers were teaching. Coming up with a test which is equally valid for all students in the classroom of a single teacher is difficult enough, let alone coming up with a test that is equally valid for all teachers in a grade in an entire school system. A test must be long enough to be reliable, and the items must be at about the right levels of difficulty so that they reveal differences among the students (if the test is too hard or too easy it will not be very useful, because all of the students will fail or pass). A test also should measure what the teachers are teaching (or, to put it another way, the learning objectives which the students are supposed to master).

In a small scale evaluation project, such problems would be solved by getting teachers to agree that all would strive to accomplish certain common objectives, and then constructing a *criterion referenced test* to assess their success in accomplishing these objectives. Criterion referenced tests are so-called because they sample student mastery of previously specified criteria or objectives. Thus, a criterion referenced spelling test would include only words which all teachers included in their spelling lessons (either all of the words or a sample of them). Such a test would be equally valid or fair for all of the teachers included in the study, because all had taught the same words.

In contrast, a test containing one hundred "fifth grade level" words would be differentially fair or valid for different fifth grade teachers, depending upon what percentage of these words had actually been taught in their classrooms. Teachers who happened to teach a greater percentage of these words to their students would have an advantage, on the average, over teachers who happened to teach a smaller percentage of these words.

Although criterion referenced tests are ideal in many ways, particularly for testing students taught by a small group of teachers who all participated in and agreed upon the selection of a specified set of objectives, they have some drawbacks. One is that they are time consuming to construct and they require agreement among the participating teachers. Another is that they are restricted to the range of objectives agreed upon, so that they do not take into account other possible objectives and they do not provide much information about the success of the group of teachers being studied relative to that of teachers in general. The latter information must come from *norms*, and these in turn come from *norm referenced tests*.

Norm referenced tests are constructed by sampling curricula used at a particular grade level, gradually compiling a test by adding good items and weeding out bad ones, then administering the test to a large number of children representative of the population of children at that grade. The scores of the children used in this norming sample then are used to establish norms for the grade. For example, if the *average* child in the fifth month of third grade scores 42 on a particular arithmetic computation test, the table of norms established to go with the test will specify that a score of 42 is equal to a "grade level equivalent score" of 3.5 (grade three, fifth month). Thus, a child achieving a score of 42 on this particular test would be said to be at, below, or above "grade level," depending upon how far along in school he was when he took the test.

Such norm referenced tests have many advantages, which is why they have been used so heavily as criteria for how a particular child or school system is doing. However, it must be remembered that they are no better than their *validity*. To the extent that they include items which were not included in the school curriculum, they are invalid. To put it another way, they are valid only insofar as they test students' mastery of objectives that teachers actually attempted to teach (or were supposed to teach).

Although they have been criticized on a variety of grounds, norm referenced tests appear to be generally valid as evaluation devices for the early elementary grades. This is because there is high agreement upon the importance of the fundamental tool skills in language arts and arithmetic, and therefore the items included on these tests tend to be items which are included in the various curricula that are used in different schools across the country. While these curricula differ considerably from one another in the amounts and kinds of media they use and in their approaches to teaching, their objectives (what they are trying to teach) are relatively constant in the early grades. These include phonics and other word attack skills and rudimentary comprehension skills in reading and language arts, and basic numerical operations in mathematics.

The criteria used in this study were the language arts and mathematics tests from the Metropolitan Achievement Tests. This test battery, which is one of the more comprehensive and widely known of the standardized achievement test batteries, had been in use for many years in the school district. Thus, although the data came from a widely known norm referenced test, the nature of the curricula in use in the school district at the time (traditional curricula published by the major distributors of elementary school curricula and widely used in the country at large), in combination with the fact that the same test had been given every fall for many years, so that the teachers were familiar with it, gave the test some of the advantages typically found in criterion referenced tests. That is, it probably was as good a test as any for testing mastery of the objectives that the teachers were in fact attempting to teach.

However, this does not mean that the test was ideal or even that it was equally applicable to all schools. In fact, recognizing this, the school district administered two different versions of the test. In most schools, the students were tested with the version of the test constructed for their particular grade levels. These students were in schools serving primarily middle and upper class populations. In contrast, students in schools serving primarily lower class populations received easier tests. These were published by the same company and were similar in general format and content to the other tests, but they were pitched at a level approximately one grade level below the tests used in the other schools.

The schools using these easier tests were the so-called "Title I" schools. These schools have student populations which contain large proportions of students from poor families, so that the schools are eligible for special equipment and financial assistance under Title I of the Educational Assistance Act. Thus, although all tests were part of the same series published by the same company, different tests were used for each of the two grades, and, within grades, different tests were used in Title I versus non-Title I schools. This evaluation plan used by the school district retained the advantages of norm referenced tests but overcame some of their disadvantages by selecting from the versions available those tests most appropriate for the students in a given school.

Test data were available on three language arts subtests (word knowledge, word discrimination, and reading), and on two arithmetic subtests (arithmetic computation and arithmetic reasoning). Thus, data were available on the two major aspects of the early elementary school curriculum, and within each of these two general areas, on separate subtests.

Given the considerations discussed above, we believe that these test data provided good information for use in measuring teacher effectiveness in producing student learning gains. However, it should be noted again that the tests measured *only* student learning gains; they provided no information about teacher success in affective areas (promotion of personal and social growth in students).

We were not particularly concerned about this at first, partly because we assumed that teacher behavior which promoted cognitive growth would also promote affective growth. Also, despite agreement about the importance of the affective area, there are no tests available which are widely accepted as valid measures of affective development, particularly not tests designed for use with young children.

However, because our first year data indicated that we might have been incorrect in assuming that teacher behavior which fosters cognitive growth also will foster affective growth, we added an affective measure in the second year of the study. This was the Student Evaluation of Teacher (SET II) test, a measure developed by the Research and Development Center for Teacher Education at the University of Texas at Austin. This test was designed specifically for use with young elementary school children as a measure of attitudes towards their teachers. Pilot work with it had shown good reliability and validity (Haak, Kleiber, and Peck, 1972). However, it did not work with the children in the classes in which we were observing.

Their patterns of responses, and the correlations between their responses and other data, were so confusing and contradictory that we do not believe that the data validly reflect student attitudes towards their teachers. Instead, they appear to reflect situational influences, yeasaying tendencies (tendency to answer "yes" to "yes-no" questions), and other irrelevant influences. Thus, we do not have direct measures of student attitudes toward teachers or of any other aspect of student affect. However, indirect inferences concerning student affect can be made from some of the observational data.

Adjusting Student Learning Scores

Student achievement progress was measured in yearly gain scores, or the differences in scores from one fall as compared to the next fall. Thus, a student whose grade level equivalent score was second grade, fifth month when he was tested in second grade and whose grade level equivalent score was third grade, ninth month when he was tested in third grade would have a raw gain score of one year and four months. However, these raw gain scores had to be adjusted before they could be used as measures of teacher effectiveness. This is accomplished through a statistical technique known as covariance analysis, and the adjusted scores are technically known as residual gain scores.

Basically, the statistical technique involves computing

an "expected gain score" for each student, and then adjusting his actual gain score according to whether it is higher than, equal to, or lower than his expected gain score. The need for this kind of adjustment arises because, on the average, elementary school students who enter a given school year with relatively high achievement scores will gain more in that year than students who enter with relatively low achievement scores (high achievers usually learn more in a given time than low achievers). As a result, a teacher working with primarily high ability students would have an unfair advantage over a teacher working with primarily low ability students if raw gain scores were used, because the high ability students will gain more on the average than the low ability students, even though the quality of teaching might be equivalent.

The use of adjusted scores avoids this problem and makes it possible to make comparisons among teachers working with students of different ability levels. Instead of simple comparisons of mean raw score gains, which confound teacher effects with student abilities, comparisons of mean *adjusted* gains which statistically control for student ability differences allow meaningful evaluations of teacher effectiveness to be made. The basis for comparison is expected gain rather than raw gain. A teacher whose students' gains averaged just about what would be expected for students in their ability level category would be considered average in effectiveness. In contrast, a teacher whose students gained less than would have been expected on the basis of their achievement scores in the fall would be considered relatively less effective, and a teacher whose students gained more than would have been expected on the basis of their achievement scores in the fall would be considered relatively more effective. Thus, technically, in this study teacher effectiveness was defined as the ability to produce learning gains which exceeded the gains to be expected on the basis of the students' achievement test scores taken in the fall at the beginning of the school year. Students in the classes of highly effective teachers gained more than expected, while students in the classes of less effective teachers gained less than expected (even though they did gain in the absolute sense).

Identifying Consistent Teachers

In preparation for the main study, teacher effectiveness scores were calculated for each of three consecutive school years on each of the subtests for which data were available. On each subtest, the mean adjusted gain score for each teacher's class was computed for the school years 1967-68, 1968-69, and 1969-70. First, adjusted gain scores were computed for each individual student within each subtest, within each of the three separate years, and also within sex. This last control was necessary because girls typically gain more than boys in the early elementary grades. Separate calculations also were made for the Title I vs. the non-Title I schools, because of the different test batteries used. Details of these calculations can be found in Brophy (1972, 1973, 1974) and Veldman and Brophy (1974).

After the data had been separated this way in order to calculate adjusted gain scores for individual students, they were put back together again to calculate a mean or average adjusted gain score on each subtest for each year for each of 88 second grade teachers and 77 third grade teachers. These 165 teachers included all teachers in the school district who had taught at either second or third grade, respectively, for each of the three years under study. Each teacher then had a mean adjusted gain score for each subtest for each of the three years, and these data were analyzed to assess the degree of consistency from year to year in the relative sizes of student gains that the teachers achieved.

This study of the *degree of consistency in teacher effectiveness*, which was conducted prior to our search for teacher behavior correlated with teacher effectiveness, was an important and purposeful step in our research plan, not just something done out of curiosity. One reason was simply to show that teachers did indeed have demonstrable effects on student learning. Recall that the Coleman report and other well-publicized studies in education had suggested that teachers had no important effects. These studies, which used schools rather than individual teachers as the unit of analysis, had shown repeatedly that measures relating to teachers did not add anything to the predictability of student learning that was not already included in a measure of student abilities or social class background.

Although other interpretations are possible, one of the more common interpretations of these findings has been that teachers do not have significant, measurable effects on student learning; that a student's learning is pretty much dependent on his ability and background, regardless of the quality of teaching at his school. Thus, one important goal in this early phase of our research was to analyze the learning gains of students grouped by class within schools rather than grouped by schools, thus studying the effectiveness of individual teachers compared with one another rather than trying to study the effectiveness of whole schools. These analyses did indeed indicate that teachers have differential effects upon student learning, and that these effects are both statistically and practically significant (Veldman and Brophy, 1974). Independent work by another investigator, using similar methods, has corroborated these findings (Acland, 1974).

In addition to establishing differential effectiveness among the teachers, we wanted to investigate the degree to which teachers were consistent across male and female students, across the different subtests used, and particularly across time (one year to the next) in their relative effectiveness in producing student learning gains. This information would have been of some interest and relevance to the study under any circumstances. However, it turned out to be crucial because of the findings and implications of research conducted by Rosenshine (1970). After reviewing studies that related teacher behavior to student learning conducted up to that time, Rosenshine could find only five which contained any information about stability or consistency in teacher effectiveness over time with different groups of students. Furthermore, the five studies that were available indicated that there was little if any stability in teacher effectiveness (as measured by student learning gains) from one semester or year to the next. Most correlations not only were not significant; they were near zero. Even those which were significant were relatively weak.

Rosenshine's data posed a fundamental threat to the whole idea of studying teachers to identify effective teaching, or at least to the idea that certain teachers are generally and consistently more effective than others. If his data accurately represented the typical or general case, terms like "master teacher" or "effective teacher" would have no meaning at all. A teacher who was very successful this year would be no more likely to be better than average next year than a teacher who was notably unsuccessful this year, and vice versa!

However, there were some reasons to believe that Rosenshine's data might not represent the more general situation accurately. First, one of the studies he reviewed involved Air Force instructors teaching short military courses to new recruits. Obviously, this situation is considerably different from that of the typical teacher teaching typical students in elementary and secondary schools. Second, two of the other studies included in this review came from a project in which teachers were implementing an innovative curriculum. Because the curriculum was innovative, the teachers necessarily were changing their previous behavior and adopting new behavior according to the instructions of the curriculum designers. Under these circumstances, in which teachers were in the process of changing their methods by dropping some old ones and adding some new ones, low stability of effectiveness (or of classroom behavior, for that matter) would be expected. Thus, three of the five studies included in Rosenshine's review involved teacher samples which were not representative of typical teachers working under ordinary conditions with typical students.

The remaining two studies did appear to be typical in this sense. However, curricula and teaching experience were not controlled. It is possible that curriculum innovations or changes were going on that might have reduced teacher stability from one year to the next, and it is not only possible but probable that the teacher samples in these studies contained numerous teachers who were starting their teaching careers. First year teachers are known to be unstable in their classroom behavior across time, because they are learning on the job. Consequently, there is no reason to expect them to show stable effects upon students until they settle into a stable pattern of teaching after they have had a chance to experiment with various methods.

Taking the above into consideration, we concluded that the most appropriate way to study stability of teacher effectiveness would be to use *experienced teachers* working with their regular students under ordinary conditions; to compare effectiveness across time periods long enough (a semester, or better yet, a full year) to allow teacher effects to appear if in fact they were present; to use adjusted gain scores in order to statistically control for differences in student ability; and to use the individual teacher as the unit of analysis, thus comparing teachers rather than schools or other groups of teachers which mask individual differences. Fortunately, the necessary data to conduct such a study were available because the school district administered the Metropolitan Achievement Tests to elementary students every fall. After collecting and collating all of the relevant data and performing the necessary statistics (as described previously), we ultimately came up with mean adjusted gain scores for each teacher for male and female students (separately and for the class a whole) for each of the subtests and for each of the three years included in the study. These data then were analyzed for consistency. The results are summarized briefly below.

First, restricting the study to experienced teachers and analyzing by teacher rather than by clusters of teachers did indeed make a difference in the findings. The correlations (stability coefficients) relating teacher success in producing student learning gains one year compared to success in producing student learning gains the next year were statistically significant for the most part and were considerably higher than most of those reported in the studies reviewed by Rosenshine (1970). It should be stated emphatically though, that these correlations were *not* high enough to justify the use of student learning gains, even if scores are adjusted for student ability, as teacher accountability devices. That is, the correlations were high enough to indicate that stability of teacher effectiveness, at least among experienced teachers, is higher than the data in the studies reviewed by Rosenshine suggested, and there were enough stable teachers in the sample of 165 to enable us to follow through with our plan to concentrate on teachers who were consistent across time in their relative effectiveness. However, the correlations were moderate rather than high, indicating among other things that it would be unfair and inappropriate to use student learning gains on standardized achievement tests as the basis for making decisions about teacher promotion, tenure, pay raises, etc.

These data are but one aspect of the larger problem concerning the teacher accountability movement; it is perhaps a logical idea on paper, but it is impractical in practice, at least at present. Introducing a merit system which would reward teachers differentially on the basis of their success in achieving relevant educational goals would probably improve the quality of teaching by providing added incentives for teachers to improve their skills. However, the present state of teacher education and educational research is such that there is no valid and fair method for doing this.

Furthermore, there will not be such a method until and unless a fund of valid and reliable information concerning the relationships between teacher behavior and student outcomes is built up. If and when this happens, we can expect to see teachers become more and more stable in their behavior in certain situations, and consequently more and more stable in their relative effectiveness. At the moment, however, knowledge about the relationships between teacher behavior and student outcomes is rather limited and primitive, so that attempts to use it as the basis for teacher accountability decisions are invalid and inappropriate. Making such decisions upon even less appropriate criteria such as unreliable supervisor or principal ratings or the degree to which the teacher follows the latest educational fad is even more unfair. Thus, for the moment, the teacher accountability idea cannot be put into practice. For a detailed discussion of this and related matters, see Good, Biddle, and Brophy (1975).

Our study of stability in teacher effectiveness produced several interesting findings. First, as mentioned above, stability was higher than previously suspected, and there were enough stable teachers in the total of 165 for us to concentrate our later observational research on teachers who showed stability across time (as well as across sex of student and subtests of the Metropolitan battery). We were pleased with this, because it seemed to us that teachers who were experienced in teaching at their grade level and who were relatively consistent in their degree of success in producing student learning gains probably also would be teachers most likely to be stable and consistent in their teaching behavior. In contrast, inexperienced teachers and teachers who showed great variability from one year to the next in their degree of success in producing student learning gains seemed more likely to be less consistent in their everyday teaching behavior, and thus to be less appropriate as a sample of teachers to use in the study designed to identify relationships between teacher behavior and student learning. For these reasons, we selected teachers who were most consistent as the teachers to concentrate on in our observational study.

Several other findings from this initial study are worth noting here. First, although girls generally showed greater gains than boys, which is typical for studies of achievement in the early elementary grades in our country, few teachers showed consistent differences in their degree of success with boys vs. girls when adjusted scores were compared. Only four of the 165 teachers consistently produced higher gains in one sex than in the other across time and subtests (two did better with boys and two with girls). Thus, although it is common for teachers to have a reputation among students in a school as favoring boys or favoring girls, teachers who regularly showed measurably greater success in producing learning gains in one sex than in the other were rare.

Similarly, analyses of the adjusted gain scores on the various subtests revealed that very few teachers were consistently more successful in language arts than in mathematics, or vice versa. Although most teachers will express a preference for one of these areas over the other, the data showed that the majority of teachers were not consistently more successful at one than the other. To put it another way, although teachers differed among themselves in their relative success, these differences tended to be rather general across subject matter areas. A teacher who consistently got good gains in language arts ordinarily got good gains in mathematics also, and a teacher who consistently got poor gains in language arts usually got poor gains in mathematics. Few teachers consistently got better gains in one of these subject areas than in the other.

Finally, a finding which relates back to the accountability issue raised above was that correlations of mean adjusted gain scores across subtests but within the same year usually were considerably higher than correlations across years for the same subtests. Thus, even though statistical procedures which theoretically take student differences into account had been applied in adjusting the scores, there was a general "class" or "cohort" effect observable when scores from one year were compared with scores from another. Teachers who were relatively high on a particular subtest in one year were likely to be high in all the other subtests in that same year, and if they were low on one subtest the next year, they also were likely to be low on the other subtests the next year. Thus, certain factors were operating to make teachers *generally* more effective or less effective one year than the next. These differences were reduced in the relatively consistent teachers as compared to the inconsistent ones, but they were observable in all of the teachers.

The causes for these "class" or "cohort" effects are unknown. Theoretically, they could include anything that might affect a teacher or class during the course of one school year, but which would make no difference or would have a different kind of effect the following year. These could include such things as the teacher's health, aspects of personal life that might affect teaching favorably or unfavorably, the number of students in the classroom, changes in curricula or methods, or characteristics peculiar to a specific class of students (achievement motivation, morale, leadership, etc.). In any case, it was clear that factors like these were operating to enhance or depress teachers' general effectiveness each year, and that their effects were observable even when student learning scores were adjusted to take into account student progress at the beginning of the school year. The existence of these "class" or "cohort" effects is another argument against using student learning as an accountability device, at least until enough is learned about such effects and what causes them to allow evaluators to systematically take them into account in evaluating teachers.

Selecting Teachers for Study

The nature of the findings reported above made it easy for us to identify teachers to be included in the following observational study, compared to the problems that might have faced us if there had been systematic teacher effectiveness differences according to sex of student and/or language arts vs. mathematics. Because relative success was general across subtests and sexes, we only had to eliminate the few teachers who showed consistent differences in these areas and then pick the teachers who showed the most generalized consistency across time for inclusion in the observational study. We were able to pick teachers on the basis of their relative consistency in producing student learning gains across the five subtests and across three consecutive years of teaching in the same grade. No absolute criterion was used. Instead, teachers were selected on the basis of their *relative* consistency across sex and subject matter and across three consecutive years of teaching.

Most of the teachers selected were consistent in both the relative and absolute sense. That is, their relative success in producing student learning gains was similar across subtests and across each of the three years included in the data. A smaller group of teachers who showed a different kind of consistency also were included in the study. These were teachers who showed a consistent *trend* of improvement or decline in relative success. These teachers gradually and consistently gained or dropped in relative effectiveness from one year to the next across the three years.

Taking into account statistical requirements and available staff, we decided that a sample of about 30 teachers would be appropriate for study in the first year. These were selected from the 40 teachers who showed the greatest general consistency in the data. Several of these teachers proved to be unavailable because they had retired, were on leave, or had shifted to another grade, and a few declined to participate. As a result, we began our observational data collection with a sample of 31 teachers. These included 13 teachers in Title I schools (seven in grade two and six in grade three), and 18 teachers in non-Title I schools (ten in grade two and eight in grade three).

Twenty-eight teachers were included the second year, of whom 19 also had been included in the first year. Most of the teachers who were in the study the first year but not in the second year had to be dropped because they were transferred to a new grade, retired, or went on leave, although a few declined to participate further. The 19 holdover teachers were supplemented with nine new teachers for the second year of the study. These nine were selected by going back to the original data and identifying the 15 teachers who showed the most consistency among the group which remained after the initial 40 had been identified.

By this time we had a fourth year data set available from the 1970-1971 school year, so that these 15 teachers were consistent across four school years, although slightly less consistent than the initial group of 40 selected the previous year. Nine of these 15 eventually were included in the second year of the study. Again, some teachers could not be used due to retirement or transfer to another grade, and a few declined to participate.

The Effectiveness Criteria

Selecting effectiveness criteria to use in the observational study proved to be a sticky problem. First, we had mean residual gain scores available on several achievement test subtests for four separate years on each of the teachers (by the time the data were analyzed). This was more data than necessary, especially because the teachers were selected on the basis of consistency across time. Also, by the time we were ready to begin the observational study, the school district had decided to discontinue annual administration of the Metropolitan Achievement Tests in the fall, so that additional data from this test battery were not available from the school system. This was a system wide change in what had been a long standing policy, so that administration of these tests ourselves would have been difficult and ill-advised even if the necessary permission had been obtained and the necessary staff and equipment had been prepared. Consequently, new data on student learning were not collected.

Instead, effectiveness scores for each teacher were obtained by *averaging the four mean residual gain scores* for each class for each of the subtests for which data were available. Given that the teachers included were selected in the first place on the basis of their consistency, and given that data from four consecutive years immediately preceding the two observational years were included, the effectiveness criterion scores probably are excellent estimates of these teachers' general effectiveness relative to one another. They are estimates, however, and thus are less definitive than tests administered after each of the two observational years would have been.

Separate scores were computed for each subtest, although as noted above, teacher effectiveness was generally consistent across subtests. As a result, correlations between various teacher measures and the scores from different subtests generally were comparable across subtests. Consequently, teachers discussed in the book were discussed in terms of their *general* effectiveness, except for the very few instances in which measures showed systematic differences in their patterns of correlation with different subtests.

Readers should bear in mind, however, that these general correlations are partly a function of the nature of the sample of teachers included in the study. That is, we deliberately chose teachers who were consistent not only across time but across student sex and across the subtests of the Metropolitan battery. The latter selection criterion operated so as to make it likely that a teacher quality or behavior that correlated positively with one of the subtests would also correlate positively with the other subtests. Our general findings for the sample of 165 teachers discussed previously suggest that there would be a tendency for different subtest scores to correlated with other variables in much the same way in any case, but this tendency was exaggerated when we picked teachers on the basis of their consistency in producing student learning gains *across subtests.*

Recruiting the Teachers

Permission to conduct the study as a whole was obtained

from the school district, and permission to observe in a particular teacher's classroom was obtained from both the principal and the teacher herself (all teachers were female, and, as it happened, married). Teacher participation was solicited through personal contact. Each teacher was given the same general orientation to the study and had her questions answered as fully as possible. The decision to participate in the study was up to the teacher, and most teachers approached did agree to participate after the intent and nature of the study were explained to them. Most reported that their primary motivation was the relevance of the study and the likelihood that it would produce results that they could use to improve their own teaching.

The teachers were given a general orientation to the study which contained no false information but which omitted certain specific details which might have upset them unnecessarily or caused them to teach differently than they would have taught otherwise. Orientation began with the statements that the authors were interested in the education of young children, that this area of education has been relatively neglected in research on teaching, and that the present study was an attempt to collect information useful to teachers in general and to teachers working with young elementary school children in particular. Teachers also were told that we were specifically interested in teachers with experience at their grade level, because we saw little point in studying inexperienced teachers in studies designed to discover how to do things most efficiently and appropriately.

The teachers were *not* informed that they were selected because of their consistency in producing student learning gains, however. We saw little point in bringing up this matter, thinking that it would serve only to upset some of the teachers. In fact, because of the sensitive nature of this information, it was and is confidential. Certain school officials and project staff members knew that the teachers had been selected on the basis of their consistency in producing student learning gains, but no one except Dr. Brophy ever had access to individual teachers' scores. Thus, although others knew that the teachers had been consistent, they did not know the specific nature of this consistency (degree of general effectiveness, rising or dropping trend).

The teachers also were given a general idea of the kinds of things that would be studied, although they were not shown coding sheets or given detailed examples of the nature of the observation systems used. They were told that the study would focus on the "bread and butter" aspects of teaching: the planning, classroom management, and teacher-student interaction that goes on everywhere, regardless of the curriculum or the nature of the school.

From the teacher's standpoint, participation in the study involved two main things: agreeing to be observed and coded periodically, and agreeing to be interviewed and to fill out questionnaires. Observations were scheduled in advance, and were intended to focus on "ordinary, everyday teaching." Unusual events such as field trips and days in which the ordinary schedule was changed because of some kind of special event were avoided. If something like this came up in between the time an appointment was made and the scheduled date, the observation was cancelled and rescheduled for a more normal day. It was stressed strongly that the role of the observer was simply to record what was going on, not to evaluate the teacher, and that the observer would be as unobtrusive as possible so that the teacher could concentrate as much as possible on teaching the way she would have taught if no observer had been present.

The interview and questionnaires were designed to measure teacher opinions on various issues thought to be important and aspects of teaching which are done outside of the classroom (or, at least, which cannot be directly observed in the classroom). The latter included such things as preparation work, testing, approaches to handling problems of individual differences, and the like. Teachers were paid $25.00 for their time spent responding to interview questions and filling out questionnaires, because this was done on their own time outside of school hours. This reimbursement money was the only direct and immediate reward that the teachers received for participating in the research.

There were indirect benefits, however. Most teachers took a certain degree of pride in being included in the study, although many of them initially were uncomfortable about being observed. Also, virtually all of the teachers enjoyed being interviewed, because (for a change!) they got a chance to give their opinions to university people who were genuinely interested in them. Unfortunately, for most of the teachers, this was the first time that anyone connected with teacher education had seriously and systematically solicited their opinions. To put it more bluntly, for most of them it was the first time that "university people" had treated them as valuable resources with important insights to offer rather than as ignorant learners in need of instruction (or worse).

The most important indirect inducement for participation in the study for most teachers, however, was provision of feedback concerning its results. Teachers were promised, and received, detailed reports of the findings, along with interpretations concerning their applications.

More information about the teachers is given in Chapter 2.

Data Collection
and Analysis Procedures

Appendix B

We believed that obtaining the teacher sample described in Appendix A was an important milestone in the development of this research, because we think this group of teachers was uniquely well suited for a study seeking to link teacher qualities with student outcomes. However, many additional decisions had to be made concerning what teacher characteristics to measure, how to measure them, and how to analyze their relationships with measures of student learning gains.

What to Study

We began the study with the intent to measure "anything" that seemed likely to correlate

with student learning gains. In practice, this meant reviewing the existing systems for classroom observation (Simon
and Boyer, 1967, 1970) and the literature on teacher effectiveness, along with drawing upon our own experiences in
working with teachers and observing in elementary school
classrooms.

Our review of existing observational systems was less
helpful than we had expected, because there is remarkable
overlap in the variables measured by different systems
(largely because "different" systems are often slight varia-
tions of the same basic original system). However, these
systems and the literature connected with them stressed the
importance of such variables as authoritarian vs. democratic
classroom leadership style, warmth and affectionateness,
enthusiasm for teaching and for the subject matter, teacher
talk vs. student talk, use of student ideas, and difficulty level
of questions. These and other variables stressed in a variety
of observation systems were included in our study, although
usually they were not measured in exactly the same way as
they are measured in other systems. This was because we
made the decision to build a single integrated and complex
system that would take into account as many variables as
possible, rather than to use a number of different systems
that overlapped considerably and that would have reduced
the data available on each variable (since observers could not
use all systems on each visit).

Most of our direction on what to study came from
reviews of teacher effectiveness literature and, more generally, the literature on curriculum and instruction and educational psychology. The teacher effectiveness literature included both presage-product studies and process-product
studies. Presage-product studies investigate the relationships
between presage variables (characteristics of students and
especially of teachers that exist independently of their classroom process behaviors, usually descriptive characteristics
such as sex or race and aspects of personality such as attitudes, expectations, and beliefs) and product variables (measures of outcomes, such as student learning gains or student
attitudes towards the teacher or the subject matter). Process-
product studies investigate the relationships between process

variables (measures of teacher and student behavior in the classroom, especially teacher-student interactions) and product variables.

The presage-product literature is disappointing, on the whole. Numerous studies have been conducted attempting to link teacher attitudes or beliefs to measures of student outcome, but the majority of these have revealed no consistent relationships or have been contradicted by other studies which failed to replicate them or even found conflicting results. Nevertheless, certain measures did appear to be important to collect, either because they appeared to be related to student outcomes or because they dealt with issues presently controversial in the field. These included such topics as attitudes toward team teaching, open classrooms, and programmed instruction; beliefs about the characteristics and needs of minority group children, beliefs about effective methods of motivating and disciplining children; and beliefs about various controversial issues in curriculum and instruction (teacher structured learning vs. discovery learning; phonics emphasis vs. whole word, sight-reading emphasis in reading instruction; homogeneous vs. heterogeneous ability grouping).

Conveniently, for us, most of the process-product literature has been summarized in books by Rosenshine (1971) and by Dunkin and Biddle (1974), and in a handbook chapter by Rosenshine and Furst (1973). These sources were very helpful (the latter sources were available to us in prepublication form when we were planning the study, even though they were not published until later). To make a long story short, these sources agree that 75 years of effort and hundreds of studies seeking to link classroom behavior measures with student outcome measures have been very disappointing. There are many reasons for this, most having to do with deficiencies in the research designs of the studies conducted. These problems are discussed in the sources mentioned above, and are analyzed in detail in Good, Biddle, and Brophy (1975).

However, while there is agreement that little progress was made for a long time, there also is agreement that studies have been improving in recent years and that at least some variables have been linked with successful student outcomes in all or most of the studies which included them, even though the relationships usually are only moderate rather than strong. These variables included such teacher character-istics as clarity in giving directions and explanations, vari-ability in teaching methods, curricula, and/or media, enthusi-asm, task oriented or business-like behavior, indirectness (questioning rather than lecturing, frequent praise, and fre-quent pupil-to-pupil interaction), student opportunity to learn material, frequent use of structuring comments, and multiple levels of questions (as opposed to concentration at only one level).

These variables generally relate positively to student outcomes, and teacher criticism generally relates negatively. This literature was extremely useful to us, even though dif-ferent writers don't always agree with one another (for example, Dunkin and Biddle are much less impressed with the data concerning the importance of variety in cognitive level of questions than are Rosenshine and Furst), and even though we sometimes disagreed with their conclusions, at least with the way that they were presented. For example, we think that the three different behaviors, described above, which usually are lumped together under the concept of "indirectness," should be measured separately.

The general literature on curriculum and instruction and educational psychology suggested other variables. For example, the controversy in early reading instruction con-cerning the relative importance of phonics vs. whole word-sight reading instruction had implications about both the gen-eral nature of reading instruction and the kinds of clues that teachers should give children when they are stuck on a word in reading group. Research on classroom mangement and behavior modification suggested that certain approaches were likely to be successful and other approaches to be unsuc-cessful. The work of Kounin (1970) on group management in the classroom was particularly useful. The literature on pro-grammed instruction suggested such variables as cueing atten-tion to relevant stimuli, sequencing the presentation of material effectively, providing opportunities for students to respond, and providing immediate feedback concerning the correctness of their responses.

Other variables stressed in the general literature which were included in the present research were the use of advance organizers to provide an optimal orientation and learning set prior to a lesson or demonstration; controversies over such matters as authoritarian vs. democratic classroom leadership styles, competitive vs. cooperative classroom atmospheres, didactic instruction vs. discovery learning; stress on the importance of individualizing instruction by adapting both objectives and methods to the student's present needs; attempting to build intrinsic motivation vs. rewarding through extrinsic reinforcement; the importance of appropriate teacher expectations and of communicating these expectations to students through appropriate behavior; the literature on praise and criticism; and many others.

Another major influence on our selection of variables and measurement techniques was our own previous research in early elementary school classrooms. In a series of studies concerning teacher expectations and attitudes done in collaboration with Thomas L. Good (summarized in Brophy and Good, 1974), we acquired considerable knowledge about the nature of schooling in general, and about teacher-student interaction in particular, at the elementary grade levels. These earlier studies were focused on teacher expectations and attitudes rather than teacher success in producing student learning gains, but the many hours of observation time spent in classrooms for the former purpose also led to a variety of ideas about what was important and how it could best be measured for the latter purpose.

The original Brophy-Good dyadic interaction observation system (Brophy and Good, 1970) had been designed specifically for research on teacher expectations and attitudes. However, during pilot work involved in putting the system together, steps were taken to design it to capture the naturalistically occurring sequences of teacher-student interactions in classrooms. Also, subsequent elaborations of the system had continued the process of refining it to make it more and more appropriate for measuring teacher-student interaction in general at these grade levels. Gradually, categories dealing with aspects of classroom process that do not occur, or occur only very rarely, in the early elementary grades were eliminated, and categories which made finer discriminations in areas that are of particular importance for the early elementary grades were added.

Other important features of the system were: it separated interactions initiated by the teacher from those initiated by the students; it took into account contextual differences such as time of day (morning vs. afternoon) and group size (whole group interaction vs. interaction in reading groups); it allowed for the retention of sequences of action and reaction during extended interchanges between teachers and students, so that particular events could be related to their antecedent causes and not merely counted; and it was based on real and psychologically meaningful units of classroom interaction (such as teacher question-student answer-teacher feedback, or student requests assistance-teacher responds), rather than on artificial units such as time samples (observing for thirty seconds, then coding for ten seconds, then observing again, etc.) which have no inherent relationship to behavior. Thus, our previous research experiences in early elementary classrooms, although conducted for a different purpose, gave us many useful insights about what to measure and how to measure it.

Finally, other personal experiences involving research with or other interaction with young children, as well as our general interest in child development and early education, gave us a special interest in the unique problems of teaching young children and some insights into the special needs of teachers who work with young children. We both have children of our own, and we have done research with preschool and early primary school children in a variety of school settings.We also have spent many hours observing and talking with teachers. These experiences led us to include certain variables in the study which had not been researched systematically before, and they made us generally aware of the fact that the existing wisdom of textbooks in curriculum and instruction and educational psychology written for teachers in general tends to be much more appropriate for teachers working in the later elementary grades or the secondary grades than for teachers working with young children in the early elementary grades. As will be noted, our findings strongly confirmed this impression.

Data Collection Instruments

Once decisions about possible variables to measure had been made and the list was reduced by eliminating redundancies, choices had to be made about how to measure the variables. Most investigators prefer, when possible, to measure class-room process variables through *low inference coding*. This method involves development of a coding system which allows the classroom observer to record the occurrence of very well-defined and objectively observable behavior or events. Presumably, low inference systems involve minimal judgment or inference on the part of the coder: The behaviors being coded are so obvious and overt that anyone given minimal training can observe and record them accurately with little difficulty.

However, some variables of interest are not quite so overt or obvious, and consequently they must be measured through high inference rating systems which require the observer to make judgments and draw inferences from a wide range of observed behaviors in order to rate the teacher as low or high on some scale. Low inference methods generally are preferred over high inference methods because high inference methods are open to the same kinds of biasing influences that make high inference ratings unreliable as measures of teacher effectiveness.

Perhaps the most important of these are halo effects and logical errors. *Halo effects* occur when an observer forms a strong positive or negative opinion about a teacher. Figuratively speaking, it is as if he sees the teacher with a halo over her head if he responds to her positively (and presumably he sees her with horns over her head if he doesn't like her!). In any case, global reactions of this kind can bias ratings, and the potential for bias increases as the rating requires the coder to infer more from what he observes. Thus, other things being equal, a rater will have a tendency to rate a teacher that he likes more positively, and to rate a teacher that he dislikes less positively, simply because of his personal reaction to her.

Logical errors occur because people tend to think that different behaviors are more strongly related to one another than they actually are. For example, suppose a rater has formed the opinion that a teacher is a warm, affectionate person. If so, he is likely to rate the teacher highly on a scale intended to measure her frequency of praise of students, since he may take it for granted that warm and affectionate teachers praise students more often than teachers who are less warm and affectionate. This may in fact be true to some degree, but it is not necessarily true of the particular teacher that he is rating. Thus, his rating of praise frequency for this teacher may be biased because of his logical error in assuming that the teacher must praise frequently because she is warm and affectionate.

These and other sources of bias in high inference ratings make them less appealing to many investigators than low inference coding, which is less subject to such biasing influences and thus is more likely to be factually accurate and "scientific." However, as Rosenshine and Furst (1973) have pointed out, low inference coding is not necessarily more valid than high inference ratings. Warmth and affectionateness are good examples. Although these qualities are difficult to define in operational and behavioral terms, they are easy to rate reliably. Apparently, this is because we "know what we mean" when we use such terms, even though we may not be able to express it in clear detail verbally, and the terms apparently have fairly constant meanings for people in general within our culture.

Consequently, high inference ratings of variables like warmth or affectionateness tend to show high agreement across different raters, even when they have been given relatively little training. In contrast, attempts to get at these varaibles through low inference coding usually have failed, even though the coding was accurate. The problem is that warmth and affectionateness are general personality variables that are expressed in a great variety of different ways. They can be perceived accurately by someone who has a chance to observe another person at some length, but they usually cannot be measured accurately by counting the frequency of certain behaviors believed to be evidence of warmth or affectionateness.

For example, it is possible to code such behaviors as

smiling, touching a child affectionately, and the like, through low inference coding, but these behaviors do not appear frequently enough and are not correlated closely enough with general warmth and affectionateness to be valid measures of these traits. Many smiles are phony or forced, and, except in the rare teacher who frequently expresses affection physically, physical touching does not occur often enough for it to be a very useful measure of warmth.

These considerations, along with practical considerations such as the upper limit on the number of things that a coder can code in a low inference fashion at one time, forced us to make decisions about how to code process behaviors observable in the classroom. The low inference coding system we ultimately used was an adaptation and expansion of the original Brophy-Good system (Brophy and Good, 1970). This system is designed so that every dyadic interaction in which a teacher is interacting with a single individual student is coded. This sytem is especially appropriate in the early grades, because the teacher interacts with individual students much more often than she interacts with the class as a whole or with a group as such.

One aspect of coding involved sequences of teacher questions, student responses, and teacher feedback. Several things were coded in sequence when these interactions occurred. First, the method by which the child received an opportunity to respond was indicated. This was coded either as pre-select (the teacher names the child before asking the question); non-volunteer (the teacher has the children raise their hands but then calls on a child who does not have his hand up); volunteer (the teacher calls on a child with his hand up); or call out (some child calls out the answer without first being recognized by the teacher).

Then, the type of question was coded. These included process questions (why and how questions that require the child to make an extended response or explanation or to describe the processes through which one arrives at an answer); product questions (short answer, factual questions, usually beginning with who, what, where, when, how much, or how many); choice questions (yes-no questions, either-or questions, or other questions in which the response alternatives were presented to the child and he only had to choose among them); opinion questions (questions which did not have a clear cut right or wrong answer in which the child was being asked his opinion); and self questions (questions concerning personal preferences and experiences or other non-academic matters).

Next, the quality of the student's response was coded. Responses were coded as correct, part-correct, incorrect, don't know (the child actually says that he doesn't know or indicates it through shrugging his shoulders or similar gestures), or no response (the child makes no overt response at all, so that it is unclear whether he simply doesn't know the answer or whether he is thinking about it).

Finally, teacher reactions to these student responses were coded. There were several categories of teacher reactions, and certain categories could be coded in combination. Teacher reaction codes included praise, criticism, giving no feedback reaction at all (simply moving on to something or someone else without giving the child any feedback about the quality of his answer if he gave one), giving the answer, giving process feedback (providing not only the answer but explaining how you get the answer by giving the steps in the process), calling on another child to give the answer, call out (some other child calls out the answer before the teacher has a chance to do anything on her own), rephrase or clue (the teacher tries to help the child get the answer by rephrasing the question or giving him some kind of hint or clue), repeat (the teacher simply indicates that she is waiting for the answer by repeating the question or probing to see if the child knows the answer, but without giving him any help), or new question (the teacher shifts to an easier question or asks something like "Did you hear the question?" when the child has not responded correctly, or asks the child another question of equal or greater difficulty when he has answered the first one correctly). Teacher reactions to student performance when reading aloud in the reading group were coded similarly, except that this coding was kept separate from the coding of student responses to teacher questions.

Other major categories of interaction included teacher initiated and student initiated private contacts. These were further subdivided into work vs. procedural interactions. Private work interactions occurred when the teacher went around checking seat work (teacher initiated work interactions) or when students came to her for help or feedback (student initiated work interactions). Teacher behavior during such interactions was coded for praise, criticism, simple feedback (giving the child an answer or a short instruction without accompanying explanation) or process feedback (taking the time to explain something at length to a child who does not understand it).

Teacher initiated procedural interactions were situations in which the teacher asked a student to perform some task or run an errand. In addition to coding the occurrence of such interactions, observers coded whether or not the teacher presented the opportunity to perform the task as a reward or privilege given to the student and whether or not she thanked the student for doing the task. Student initiated procedural interactions occurred when the student approached the teacher for permission to get or do something. These interactions were coded for whether the student's request was granted, delayed, or not granted.

The final major category of interactions was behavioral interactions. These occurred when a teacher singled out a child for praise of his classroom behavior or, most typically, for some kind of interference with what the student was doing because the student's behavior was disruptive. The teacher was coded for "warning" if she merely warned the child that he should stop what he was doing and/or get to work, but she was coded for criticism if she went beyond a mere warning by threatening the child, criticizing him, or punishing him. In addition to these codes of the teacher's treatment of the particular child during behavior related contacts, behavior interactions were coded with several categories adapted from the work of Kounin (1970). The teacher was coded for having made a timing error if she waited too long before intervening, so that what started out as a minor problem became a major disruptive one. She was coded for a target error if she blamed the wrong child or blamed only some of the guilty parties but not others. She was coded for an "overreaction" if she showed strong anger, disgust, or other negative emotional reactions out of proportion to the seriousness of the problem. If none of these imperfections in the teacher's response to a behavioral management problem occurred, she was coded for "no error."

Behavior in these various categories was coded and tabulated separately for morning vs. afternoon interactions and for interactions occurring during reading groups. Also, the categories themselves were kept separate from one another, so that behavior occurring in different contexts could be analyzed separately. For example, praise was separately coded and tabulated as it occurred in public response opportunity situations (morning vs. afternoon vs. reading group and reading turn vs. response to teacher question), teacher initiated private contacts (work vs. procedure), child initiated private contacts (work vs. procedure), and behavior contacts. Taking context into effect in this manner proved to be important, because praise and other variables showed different relationships to student learning measures depending upon the context in which they appeared.

The above variables were considered the ones most important to code in low inference fashion in the early grades. They also comprised about as much as one coder could code reliably. Consequently, other variables were measured through high inference ratings and checklists. One instrument was designed to measure certain variables of teaching and lesson presentation occurring during structured lessons. This system addressed such variables as the use of advance organizers, the sequencing of ideas, the use of media, and the time spent in various aspects of the lesson (introductory orientation, presentation of new material, provision of opportunities for practice and getting feedback, reviewing, explaining the seatwork assignment, etc.).

Another high inference measure was a set of 12 five-point rating scales developed by Emmer and Peck (1973) on the basis of a factor analysis of five major systems of classroom interaction analysis. These scales concerned variables that traditionally have been stressed in classroom interaction analysis research (positive affect, negative affect, clarity, enthusiasm, use of student ideas, type of questions asked, etc.).

Other ratings and checklists were collected from a variety of sources to measure general teacher attributes that we thought were important and could be rated reliably through high inference methods (credibility, expectations, affectionateness, student orientation, student liking for the teacher, student respect for the teacher, etc.).

In addition to these low and high inference measures of classroom process behavior, an interview and several questionnaires were used to measure presage variables. These were administered to the 28 teachers participating in the second year and also to two teachers who had participated in the first year but then retired. Items that were focused and specific enough to be appropriate for inclusion on a checklist or questionnaire scale were included in the questionnaires. Matters which did not lend themselves well to forced choice formats as required by questionnaires were included in the interview, which allowed the teachers to respond to questions in more lengthy and open ended fashion. A unique feature of the interview was that the teachers themselves were given an opportunity to contribute to it. In addition to asking the questions that we were interested in, we asked the teachers to suggest questions for the interview which concerned matters that *they* thought were important and should be asked in a study of this kind. Several teachers did contribute questions, and these were included.

Data Tabulation and Reduction

Observations were conducted for about 10 hours in each classroom the first year, and for about 30 hours in each classroom the second year. Although a few of the low inference measures were simple frequency counts, most were constructed by creating percentage scores reflecting the frequency of some particular variable divided by the number of situations in which that variable was or could have been appropriate (for example, percentage of correct answers followed by praise; percentage of work related interactions which were initiated by the teacher rather than the student; or percentage of behavioral interventions involving mere warnings rather than more strongly negative reactions).

In the past, we have found such percentage measures to be much more psychologically meaningful than simple frequency counts, and they are especially appropriate when different teachers are being compared with one another. For example, one teacher may have had twice as many behavioral interventions as another, so that simple counts of behavioral warnings or negative reactions to misbehavior would be misleading because of this difference in the sheer frequencies of misbehavior. However, the percentage measure "warnings divided by warnings plus negative reactions" has essentially the same meaning for both teachers and allows direct comparison, even though the absolute difference in frequencies should be kept in mind in interpreting the result.

Teachers were assigned scores on the high inference rating measures by combining the ratings of two observers. Observers were trained to rate reliably and validly, but as an extra hedge against systematic rater bias, each teacher was observed by two raters. In the first year, raters worked in pairs so that both were present for all ten hours of observation (divided into four visits of two and one-half hours each, two mornings and two afternoons). In the second year, in order to get more data, raters worked in pairs until they achieved high reliability and then worked separately. However, the same pair of raters was assigned to a given teacher, more or less alternating visits to her classroom. Thus, when high inference ratings were filled out at the end of the year, each of these two raters had visited that teacher's classroom about seven times each (again, for two and one-half hour visits comprising either a whole morning or a whole afternoon), and thus both were familiar with her. The observations of both observers were taken into account by adding their ratings on high inference instruments. The high inference classroom observation scales (Emmer and Peck, 1973) were filled out one or more times on each visit, so that these data were summed and averaged. The remaining high inference instruments were filled out at the end of the year after the observers had had a chance to become quite familiar with the characteristics and styles of each of the teachers they had observed.

The questionnaire data required no transformation because scoring was predesigned. The questions were five-point scales, two-point scales involving agreement or disagreement with the item, or checklists in which an item was coded as present or absent. The interview responses, however, required considerable preparation and tabulation to arrive at usable scores. Since most of the interview questions were open ended ones, the interview could not be scored "automatically." Instead, answers to each question were analyzed for common subsets, and gradually a category system was devised for each question which allowed each teacher's answer to be coded as present or absent for each of the categories. This was done by staff members who did not know the teachers and had no knowledge of the teachers' scores on the criterion effectiveness measures. As a result, the nature of the categories they defined and the scoring of each teacher's responses could not have been influenced by knowledge of the teachers' effectiveness scores.

Eventually, several hundred responses were available from the questionnaires and the interview. In order to reduce the data, subsets of these responses were subjected to factor analyses. The usual factor analytic procedures could not be followed because we had many more items than teachers, so that items were broken down into subsets that appeared to be related on a common sense basis. Items that did combine into strong factors from these statistical analyses, and which also made psychological sense on a common sense basis, were added together to form combination scores, after applying a weighting system that allowed each item to contribute equally to the total. Items that did not cluster together with other items to form factors were analyzed separately. These analyses resulted in the inclusion of 273 questionnaire items on 62 factors, leaving 214 items to be analyzed separately. Similarly, 119 interview items were included on 44 factors, leaving 260 items of the interview to be analyzed separately.

The result of all this was a total of 580 presage variables available for analysis. The actual total of usable variables was much lower, however. Many of the presage variables showed little or no variance because most or all of the teachers either agreed or disagreed with the item, and many of the process variables showed little or no variance simply because they didn't occur at all or often enough to allow meaningful analyses to be performed. A total of 50 presage variables in the second year and 212 process variables in each year could not be analyzed for their relationship to teacher effectiveness criteria because of low variance or low N.

Data Analyses

Once the presage and process data were reduced to the point where the scores that we intended to use were available, they were ready for analysis of their relationships (if any) to the criteria of teacher effectiveness (mean adjusted gain scores on the subtests of the Metropolitan battery). Two basic methods were used: correlational analyses and multilinear curve fitting regression analyses. The correlational analyses are more familiar and traditional. These yield Pearson product moment correlation coefficients (r's) which indicate linear relationships between variables. Only linear relationships are taken into account with this measure; it is not sensitive to nonlinear relationships (see Figure B-1).

FIGURE B-1. Schematic linear relationships between teacher behavior and student learning

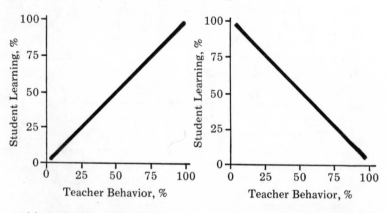

(a) A positive relationship, in which student learning increases in direct proportion to increases in a particular teacher behavior.

(b) A negative relationship, in which student learning decreases in direct proportion to increases in a particular teacher behavior.

In contrast, the multilinear curve fitting regression analyses were specifically designed to reveal nonlinear relationships between presage or process variables and student outcome variables, as well as to reveal differences in the nature of these relationships between teachers working in low SES schools vs. teachers working in high SES schools. There are a great number of possible linear and nonlinear relationships that can be revealed through such analyses (see Figure B-2), although perhaps the most interesting and important is the so-called "inverted U" curvilinear relationship discussed by Soar (1972).

In this relationship, the most successful teachers show an optimal medium level on the presage or process measure. Less successful teachers show either too much or too little of the presage or process variable. Such a relationship indicates that the successful teachers are moderate with regard to this particular variable, while the less successful teachers

FIGURE B-2. Schematic non-linear relationships between teacher behavior and student learning

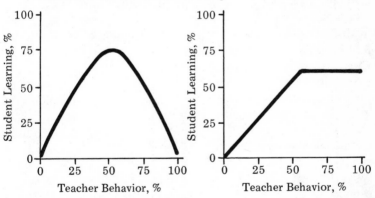

(a) An "inverted U" relationship, in which student learning is greatest when the teacher behavior is at an optimal level, neither too low nor too high.

(b) A non-linear relationship. The teacher behavior is positively related to student learning up to a point (50% in this case), but beyond this point, increases in the teacher behavior do not produce further increases in student learning.

tend to be at either extreme, being either very low or very high. Soar has been arguing the importance of checking for such relationships for some time, and other writers have explicitly or implicitly suggested their importance. For example, Hunt (1961), with his concept of matching educational input to the student's present level of ability and motivation, and Ausubel (1963), with his statement that the most important determinant of learning is the present status of the learner, among others, both imply such a curvilinear relationship between input and student readiness.

Material which is too easy because the student already knows it will not benefit him much, and material which is too difficult for him to learn at this time will not benefit him much, either. In contrast, material which is sufficiently familiar for him to handle but also sufficiently challenging to move him up to higher levels of learning is optimal for him. Thus, difficulty of material relates curvilinearly to student learning. This kind of relationship has been suggested for several other variables, also, but educational researchers typically have not *systematically* analyzed their data in order to discover them. The present study is an exception to this historical trend and hopefully the beginning of a new trend featuring such analyses as a standard approach to the problems in this area.

Initial analyses of the relationships between presage or process variables and student outcome variables revealed that grade was of little or no significance but that student social class was. Consequently, the data were analyzed separately by social class in addition to being analyzed for the total sample in each of the two years. In the first year, the analyses were done for Title I schools vs. non-Title I schools. In the second year, in order to come up with a somewhat closer balance, the schools were divided at the median on a measure of social status of the school population that was obtained by having six school district administrators independently rate the schools on a seven-point scale of SES. These ratings, which were highly intercorrelated (r's all above .90), were summed to obtain a single social status measure for each school, and this measure was then used as the basis for splitting the data into low SES vs. high SES subgroups.

These separate analyses by social class subgroups proved to be extremely important, because, as noted frequently throughout the book, the data generally make more sense for the SES subgroups separately than they do for the sample as a whole. That is, there are numerous differences between what is optimal for teaching in low SES schools vs. teaching in high SES schools. Some of these relationships are merely different, and some are flatly contradictory (i.e., what is good for one type of student is bad for another type, and vice versa).

The findings presented in this book, unless otherwise indicated, have been confined to the strongest ones, especially those which appeared consistently across several measures and criterion scores. Numerous findings which were statistically significant (at $p = .10$ or below) have been omitted because they were isolated findings of questionable meaning and significance and/or because they failed to replicate across the two years of the study. Readers interested in the full details should consult the references listed in Appendix C.

Annotated Bibliography

Appendix C

Readers who desire detailed reports of the research method and results discussed in the book should consult the following sources:

Brophy, J. Stability in teacher effectiveness. (Res. Rep. 77). Austin, Texas: Research and Development Center for Teacher Education, 1972. (ERIC No. ED 066 438).
This is a basic research report on the initial study, designed to evaluate the degree to which teachers are consistent across years, sex of students, and subtests in their relative effectiveness in producing student learning gains. Both the statistical design and analyses and the results are presented in lengthy detail.

Brophy, J. Stability of teacher effectiveness. *American Educational Research Journal*, 1973, 10, 245-252.
This is a briefer report based upon the preceding one. It presents considerable detail about the statistical design and methods used in identifying consistent teachers, as well as summary data concerning the results of this investigation.

Brophy, J. and Evertson, C. Low-inference observational coding measures and teacher effectivenesss. *Catalog of Selected Documents in Psychology*, 1973(a), 3, 97. (ERIC No. ED 077 879).

This is a detailed report containing the Pearson product moment correlations between low inference measures of classroom process behaviors (teacher-student interaction) and student learning criteria. This report covers the first year of the study only.

Brophy, J. and Evertson, C. Appendix to first-year data of Texas teacher effectivenesss project: Complex relationships between teacher process variables and student outcome measures. *Catalog of Selected Documents in Psychology*, 1973(b), 3, 137. (ERIC No. ED 095 173).

This report presents both the linear and non-linear relationships between low and high inference measures of classroom process (teacher-student interaction) and student learning measures. Again, only data from the first year of study are included.

Brophy, J. and Evertson, C. Process-product correlations in the Texas teacher effectiveness study: Final report. (Res. Rep. 74-4). Austin, Texas: Research and Development Center for Teacher Education, 1974(a). (ERIC No. ED 091 394).

This report, parallel to the Brophy and Evertson, 1973(a) report listed above, presents the Pearson correlations between measures of classroom process (both high and low inference) and measures of student learning. Data from both years of the project are included and are discussed in relation to one another.

Brophy, J. and Evertson, C. The Texas teacher effectiveness project: Presentation of nonlinear relationships and summary discussion. (Res. Rep. 74-6). Austin, Texas: Research and Development Center for Teacher Education, 1974(b). (ERIC No. ED 099 345).

This report, parallel to the Brophy and Evertson (1973b) report listed above, presents the linear and nonlinear relationship between both low and high inference measures of classroom process behavior (teacher-student interaction) and student learning measures. Again, data from both years are discussed and integrated.

Evertson, C. and Brophy, J. High-inference behavioral ratings as correlates of teaching effectiveness. *Catalog of Selected Documents in Psychology*, 1973, 3, 97. (ERIC No. ED 095 174).

This report presents the linear Pearson correlations between high inference coder ratings of teacher-student interaction and measures of student learning. The data included in this report are restricted to those for the high inference ratings taken during only the first year of the two years of the project.

Evertson, C. and Brophy, J. Texas teacher effectiveness project: Questionnaire and interview data. (Res. Rep. 74-5). Austin, Texas: Research and Development Center for Teacher Education, 1974. (ERIC No. ED 099 346).

This report presents the linear Pearson correlations between variables taken from the teacher questionnaire and interview data and measures of student learning. These data were taken from the 28 teachers included in the second year of the study, along with two teachers who had been included in the first year of the study but who had retired in the meantime.

Veldman, D. and Brophy, J. Measuring teacher effects on pupil achievement. *Journal of Educational Psychology*, 1974, 66, 319-324.

This report expands upon the Brophy (1972, 1973) reports listed above dealing with the data from the original study concerning stability of teacher effectiveness. It concentrates less on stability and more on the question of statistically significant teacher effects, showing that the teachers had effects which were both statistically and practically significant even when student achievement was controlled by using student scores from one year as covariables in adjusting their scores for the following year.

References

Acland, H. 1974. The consistency of teachers' impact upon pupil learning: Part I. Cambridge: The Huron Institute, (mimeographed report).

Ausubel, D. 1963. *The psychology of meaningful verbal learning.* New York: Grune and Stratton.

Brophy, J. 1972. Stability in teacher effectiveness. (Res. Rep. 77). Austin, Texas: Research and Development Center for Teacher Education, (ERIC No. ED 066 438).

Brophy, J. 1973. Stability of teacher effectiveness. *American Educational Research Journal,* **10**, 245-252.

Brophy, J. 1974. Achievement correlates. In H. Walberg (ed.). *Evaluating educational performance: A source book of methods, instruments, and examples.* Berkeley: McCutchan.

Brophy, J. and Evertson, C. 1973(a). Low-inference observational coding measures and teacher effectiveness. *Catalog of Selected Documents in Psychology,* 3, 97. (ERIC No. ED 077 879).

Brophy, J. and Evertson, C. 1973(b). Appendix to first-year data of Texas teacher effectiveness project: Complex relationships between teacher process variables and student outcome measures. *Catalog of Selected Documents in Psychology*, 3, 97. (ERIC No. ED 095 173).

Brophy, J. and Evertson, C. 1974(a). Process-product correlations in the Texas teacher effectiveness study: Final report. (Res. Rep. 74-4). Austin, Texas: Research and Development Center for Teacher Education. (ERIC No. ED 091 394).

Brophy, J. and Evertson, C. 1974(b). The Texas teacher effectiveness project: Presentation of nonlinear relationships and summary discussion. (Res. Rep. 74-6). Austin, Texas: Research and Development Center for Teacher Education. (ERIC No. ED 099 345).

Brophy, J. and Good, T. 1970. The Brophy-Good dyadic interaction system. In A. Simon and E. Boyer (eds.). *Mirrors for behavior: An anthology of observation instruments continued, 1970 supplement*, Volume A. Philadelphia: Research for Better Schools, Inc.

Brophy, J. and Good, T. 1974. *Teacher-student relationships: Causes and consequences.* New York: Holt, Rinehart and Winston.

Coleman, J. et *al.* 1966. *Equality of educational opportunity.* Washington, D.C.: Superintendent of Documents, U.S. Government Printing Office.

Crawford, J. 1975. An examination of the effect of error rates and grade point average on learning gains. Paper presented at the annual meeting of the Southwestern Psychological Association.

Cronbach, L. 1967. How can instruction be adapted to individual differences? In R. Gagne (ed.). *Learning and individual differences.* Columbus, Ohio: Merrill.

Dunkin, M. and Biddle, B. 1974. *The study of teaching.* New York: Holt, Rinehart and Winston.

Emmer, E. and Peck, R. 1973. Dimensions of classroom behavior. *Journal of Educational Psychology*, 64, 223-240.

Evertson, C. and Brophy, J. 1973. High-inference behavioral ratings as correlates of teaching effectiveness. *Catalog of Selected Documents in Psychology*, 3, 97. (ERIC No. ED 095 174).

Evertson, C. and Brophy, J. 1974. Texas teacher effectiveness project: Questionnaire and interview data. (Res. Rep. 74-5). Austin, Texas: Research and Development Center for Teacher Education. (ERIC No. ED 099 346).

Faunce, R. 1970. Teacher attitudes toward culturally disadvantaged children. Paper presented at the annual meeting of the American Educational Research Association.

Flanders, N. 1970. *Analyzing teacher behavior.* Reading, Mass.: Addison-Wesley.

Francis, E. 1975. Grade level and task difficulty in learning by discovery and verbal reception methods. *Journal of Educational Psychology,* 67, 146-150.

French, E. 1958. Effects of the interaction of motivation and feedback on task performance. In J. Atkinson (ed.). *Motives in fantasy, action, and society.* New York: Van Nostrand Reinhold.

Good, T., Biddle, B., and Brophy, J. 1975. *Teachers make a difference.* New York: Holt, Rinehart and Winston.

Good, T. and Brophy, J. 1971. Analyzing classroom interaction: A more powerful alternative. *Educational Technology,* 11, 36-41.

Good, T. and Grouws, D. 1975. Teacher rapport: Some stability data. *Journal of Educational Psychology,* 67, 179-182.

Haak, R., Kleiber, D., and Peck, R. 1972. Student evaluation of teacher instrument, II. Test Manual. Austin, Texas: Research and Development Center for Teacher Education.

Hambleton, R. 1974. Testing and decision-making procedures for selected individualized instructional programs. *Review of Education Research,* 44, 371-400.

Hughes, D. 1973. An experimental investigation of the effects of pupil responding and teacher reacting on pupil achievement. *American Educational Research Journal,* 10, 21-37.

Hunt, J. 1961. *Intelligence and experience.* New York: Ronald Press.

Kounin, J. 1970. *Discipline and group management in classrooms.* New York: Holt, Rinehart and Winston.

Meissner, J. 1975. Use of relational concepts by inner-city children. *Journal of Educational Psychology,* 67, 22-29.

Ragosta, M., Soar, R., Soar, R., and Stebbins, L. 1971. Sign vs category: Two instruments for observing levels of thinking. Paper presented at the annual meeting of the American Educational Research Association.

Rosenshine, B. 1970. The stability of teacher effects upon student achievement. *Review of Educational Research,* 40, 647-662.

Rosenshine, B. 1971. *Teaching behaviours and student achievement.* London: NFER.

Rosenshine, B. and Furst, N. 1973. The use of direct observation to study teaching. In R. Travers (ed.). *Second handbook of research on teaching.* Chicago: Rand McNally.

Rosenthal, R. and Jacobson, L. 1968. *Pygmalion in the classroom.* New York: Holt, Rinehart and Winston.

Rowe, M. 1972. Wait-time and rewards as instructional variables: Their influence on language, logic and fate control. Paper presented at the annual meeting of the National Association for Research in Science Teaching.

Siegel, M. and Rosenshine, B. 1972. Teacher behavior and student achievement in the DISTAR program. *Chicago Principal's Reporter,* 62, 24–28.

Simon, A. and Boyer, E. 1967. *Mirrors for behavior: An anthology of observation instruments.* Philadelphia: Research for Better Schools, Inc.

Simon, A. and Boyer, E. 1970. *Mirrors for behavior: An anthology of observation instruments continued, 1970 supplement,* Volumes A and B. Philadelphia: Research for Better Schools, Inc.

Soar, R. 1972. Teacher behavior related to pupil growth. *International Review of Education,* 18, 508–526.

Soar, R. and Soar, R. 1974. A profile analysis of classroom behavior. Paper presented at the annual meeting of the American Educational Research Association.

St. John, N. 1971. Thirty-six teachers: Their characteristics and outcomes for black and white pupils. *American Educational Research Journal,* 8, 635–648.

Stallings, J. 1974. An implementation study of seven Follow Through models for education. Paper presented at the annual meeting of the American Educational Research Association.

Taylor, M. 1968. Intercorrelations among three methods of estimating students' attention. (Rep. Ser. 39). Stanford, California: Stanford Center for Research on Teaching.

Thompson, G. and Hunnicutt, C. The effect of praise or blame on the work achievement of "introverts" and "extroverts." *Journal of Educational Psychology,* 1944, 35, 257–266.

Turner, R. and Thompson, R. Relationships between college student ratings of instructors and residual learning. Paper presented at the annual meeting of the American Educational Research Association, 1974.

Van de Riet, H. Effects of praise and reproof on paired-associate learning in educationally retarded children. *Journal of Educational Psychology*, 1964, **55**, 139–143.

Veldman, D. and Brophy, J. Measuring teacher effects on pupil achievement. *Journal of Educational Psychology*, 1974, **66**, 319–324.

Weiner, B. and Kukla, A. An attributional analysis of achievement motivation. *Journal of Personality and Social Psychology*, 1970, **15**, 1–20.

Wright, C. and Nuthall, G. Relationships between teacher behaviors and pupil achievement in three experimental elementary science lessons. *American Educational Research Journal*, 1970, **7**, 477–491.

Name Index

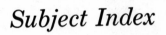

Subject Index